DISTRIBUTOR'S GUIDE TO
Analytics

Gale Media, Inc.
2569 Park Lane, Suite 200
Lafayette, CO 80026
303-443-5060
www.mdm.com

Gale Media is a market-leading information services and publishing company. Its two business units – Modern Distribution Management and MDM Analytics (formerly Industrial Market Information) – provide knowledge products and services to professionals in industrial product and wholesale distribution markets. Since 1967, MDM has been the definitive resource for distribution management best practices, competitive intelligence and market trends through its twice-monthly newsletter, market intelligence reports, books and conferences. MDM Analytics provides proprietary market research and analytic services to profile market share and account potential for industrial products.

Additional editing & layout by Eric Smith & J. Brooke Baum
Modern Distribution Management

ISBN 978-0990673811

CONTENTS

Introduction

Analytics has evolved rapidly in wholesale distribution channels, fueled in part by the explosion of technology innovation over the past several years, but also as a part of the industry's natural lifecycle. Companies that keep building their analytic capability are staying ahead of the recent waves of disruption.

The following chart provides a useful way to think about how fully a company is leveraging analytics across its three primary functions. It is widely used (and argued about) by many analytics professionals and attributed to IBM. And it is a good guidepost for thinking about how to nurture an analytics culture in your organization.

Defining Analytics

DESCRIPTIVE	PREDICTIVE	PRESCRIPTIVE
What happened?	What is likely to happen?	What should we do?
• Reporting • Dashboards • Scorecards • Segmentation • Clustering	• Data mining • Modeling • Forecasting	• Optimization • Simulation • Big data analysis
Lower	**COMPLEXITY & VALUE**	Higher

Descriptive analytics are what most distributors live and breathe – ERP exports, Excel analysis, dashboards to slightly deeper comparative tools that give visibility into what the data say happened or is happening.

Predictive analytics can't tell the future, but can combine historic data with some modeling to forecast a future state or likely outcome. Data mining can build correlations between datasets. Example: Based on your sales history of widgets into Toledo, it's possible to profile other markets or similar types of customers. Combining data from transaction history to identify likely cross-selling opportunities is another example.

Prescriptive analytics typically build on the first two levels of analytics to suggest a course of action based on why something is happening. Traditional examples include inventory optimization, pricing and profitability analysis. This is also the playground of big data. More complex models can create scenarios or alternate outcomes from larger and in some cases more unstructured data sources, such as online digital content, video, social media.

Where is your company on the spectrum of analytics adoption and thinking?

Over the past 25 years, I have had the privilege to work with and learn from some of the leading analytic thinkers in distribution, including those who generously share their knowledge in these pages. Our contributing authors have been applying analytics to solve business problems, identify opportunities and improve performance for thousands of distributors globally. Collectively, that's quite an asset, and one we have attempted to digest into a readable and easy-to-understand guide to help you think differently and analytically about transforming your company into a higher-performance one.

The strategic role of analytics and analytic thinking is changing rapidly in every industry and sector of our society, including wholesale distribution, for a single very good reason – better decision making. Companies find there is a huge return on investment in building a capability and culture based on analytic thinking. Our research indicates a widening strategic gap between distribution companies that increasingly make fact-based and data-derived decisions and those that don't.

But we still have a long way to go. In a survey conducted by Modern Distribution Management in 2013, just 12 percent of respondents said they relied on analytics for all of their sales, marketing and operational decisions. More than a third in the survey said their executives don't understand or support the use of analytics. Or they don't know where to begin.

I urge you to consider analytics capability as a strategic imperative if you aren't already, and to use the concepts collected in this book to build a vision for how to build that going forward.

I'd like to share a final thought to dispel one of the biggest myths about analytics before you dig into the insights here. Analytics is often regarded as a purely quantitative discipline, all about spreadsheets, pivot tables, statistics and algorithms. Nothing could be further from the truth.

Executives often bow too quickly to the data, without fully challenging assumptions. There is a great deal of creative thinking and qualitative evaluation that has to go into quantitative analysis for it to be successful. This is most evident in framing the analysis, determining specific questions to be answered, and selecting the appropriate methodology.

The best decision-making I have witnessed beautifully combines quantitative analysis with the intuitive knowledge about markets, competitors, customer behavior and other variables that only years of experience can create. That perspective is invaluable and it is practiced by the top market leaders in every sector of distribution, regardless of size.

I think this last point is critical to keep in mind as you read this book. Reading it won't make you an expert analyst, but it will give you the ingredients to assess and benchmark your current analytic capabilities, find some quick hits with big impact, and to start building your analytics road map and priorities.

How to Use this Book

This book is intended as a tool set, where each chapter can be used individually to improve different parts of your business. But it is also organized to give you a broader view of how and where to integrate business analytics.

You will find often complimentary, sometimes overlapping and occasionally contradictory points of view, all meant to deepen and broaden your ability to deploy analytics. That's intentional! There is no single right answer. We think you will come away with a well-rounded overview of what leading wholesale distribution companies are doing to build a significant gap between themselves and their competitors.

Share this book with your management team. It can get your team thinking about and discussing the best application of analytics for the highest return for your particular business circumstance. Assign a chapter as the basis for a meeting to discuss next steps.

Use the self-assessment tools in the final chapter to evaluate where on the analytics spectrum your team is currently, and to measure how to build priorities.

By reading this book, you will gain a better understanding of specific analytic techniques in distribution businesses today and how they are used. When you are ready to launch an analytics project, either internally or contracted, you will already know what and where the opportunities for projects are, and how to prioritize them. If you are already performing some of the analytics described here, we hope this book will give you fresh ideas and approaches for current and future projects.

Good luck and safe journey!

Thomas P. Gale

Chapter 1

Profit Analytics:
Choose the Right Variables to Measure

Dr. Albert D. Bates, Profit Planning Group

Perfection in business might be unattainable, but distributors can differentiate themselves from competitors and improve profit through thoughtful, careful analysis. Knowing which variables to measure can be a difficult process to begin, so this chapter presents the critical profit values – sales size, sales growth, gross margin percentage, operating expense percentage, days sales outstanding and inventory turnover – that will increase efficiency and improve profitability. Developing the right plan that balances these CPVs and having a management team in place that is willing to implement this plan through operational excellence and cost control will soon generate a higher profit.

To be better than the competition, the obvious approach for a distributor is doing everything better than its competitors. That is easier said than done. Actually, it is close to impossible. Of the 885 firms included in my recent research, nine had a perfect score on managing all the critical profit variables better than the typical firm in their lines of trade. The reward of doing so is high – these firms returned a profit before taxes that was, on average, 128.6 percent higher than typical – but only 1 percent of the firms could achieve it.

Even if distributors try to achieve perfection, they are unlikely to reach it. Every company has a tendency to emphasize some part of the business more than others. Some firms have a sales orientation, others emphasize asset control. This simply reflects the different perspectives of different management teams.

A critical element all distributors should emphasize to improve profitability is analytics. Distributors must analyze the appropriate variables for their business to improve overall profitability. You can try to measure and change everything, but chances are you'll end up not placing enough focus on the variables where you can achieve the best results.

Moving from "typical" to "best of breed" is a journey every firm should want to take. The challenge in driving higher profit, however, is that the correct path isn't always clear. Finding the right way is further complicated by the omnipresent "conventional wisdom." But believing something just because everyone else believes it doesn't make it actually true, and following something just because that's the way it has always been done doesn't make it a good path.

Enter analytics. A small number of performance factors drive profit, and when these critical profit variables (CPV) are combined properly, profit surges ahead. When they aren't, profit lags far behind its potential. The most fundamental profit mistake distributors make is not managing CPVs effectively – and much of that may come from not really understanding them and the role they can play in improving your bottom line.

The Search for Relationships

One of the most widely debated financial aspects of distribution management is in identifying where the most effort should be spent. Should a firm emphasize driving additional sales volume to spread overhead expenses across a larger base? Should it try to enhance gross margin percentage even if that action diminishes the level of sales growth? Should it focus on the investment side of the business to lower inventory and accounts receivable levels?

The answers depend, in large part, on the profit impact that different actions have. If sales has a greater impact on profit than gross margin percentage, then sales should be emphasized even at the expense of some margin. Before taking such action, though, it is imperative to be sure that sales really is more important than gross margin.

The task of identifying specific actions to improve performance can be approached in three very different ways. First, from an observational approach, there is the issue of seeing where most firms actually place the greatest emphasis at present. Second, financial modeling can provide insights into what should drive profit to higher levels. Finally, with an adequate sample, empirical analysis can be used to measure statistically how different actions drive profit.

Observation: It is possible to take a "wisdom of crowds" approach to seeing where management thinks the greatest payoff can be found. From this perspective, the overwhelming answer is that sales is the preferred profit driver. At any convention, the sessions on increasing sales are the biggest draws. The University of Innovative Distribution (formerly the University of Industrial Distribution), one of the premier training programs in distribution, focuses many of its sessions on some aspect of increasing sales. In 2014, a total of 17 out of 33 sessions fell into this category. It is a message that management wants and likes to hear.

The weakness of observation is that it doesn't always provide data, instead relying on assumptions and conventional wisdom. For example, an overly heavy emphasis on sales may ultimately prove dysfunctional because it ignores other factors.

Financial modeling: It is possible with programs such as Microsoft Excel, to build highly sophisticated models of distributor performance. Such models have proven to be extremely powerful tools in channeling the efforts of individual firms toward improving financial results.

Modeling inevitably comes to the conclusion that three factors are the keys to profitability. The most important is gross margin, even if the margin dollars come at the expense of sales. The second factor is expense control, followed by sales.

Modeling has the serious limitation of assuming that as one factor (e.g., gross margin) is changed, the other factors stay the same or change in a highly predictable manner. In the daily operation of distribution businesses, such precise interaction between variables seldom occurs.

Modeling is ideal for examining what could be done to improve performance, but it can't determine if high gross margin firms, in aggregate, perform better or worse than low gross margin ones. It is equally limited in analyzing any other profitability driver.

Empirical analysis: By far the most powerful approach in measuring the impact of management actions on profitability is to examine the diverse actions of a lot of companies and see how said actions actually influence profitability. While this is the most powerful approach, it is inordinately expensive and time-consuming.

The problem with any empirical analysis is the size of the sample and the extent of coverage. Generally, such inquiries are limited to publicly held companies. This inevitably limits the size of the sample, as most distributors are still private entities. Such public companies also tend to be clustered in a few industries.

There is also a quality issue in using publicly available information, such as the annual reports of public firms. Most firms want to disclose as little as possible to competitors who most certainly will scour the reports for information.

An empirical approach is ideal, but it requires the ability to expand the sample size, breadth of industries and richness of information for analysis – something that creates a challenge for agencies with a lot of experience doing this type of research. As a result, it may not be feasible for many distribution firms to undertake this initiative.

That said, if you have access to empirical analysis, such as what I will provide below, it can help overcome the weaknesses inherent in the first two measures.

Clearing the CPV Fog

As is often said in analytics, you simply can't look at everything and expect positive results across the board. "Boiling the ocean" is one way to quickly become overwhelmed. A better approach is to focus on a few CPVs to become better than typical.

There are six different CPVs that I focus on in my recent research: sales size, sales growth, gross margin percentage, operating expense percentage, days sales outstanding (DSO) and inventory turnover. One key reason why you can't expect to focus on all of these is that they sometimes don't work in tandem. For example, if you increase sales volume, you might have to sacrifice margin.

Taking three actions at a time produces 20 different CPV combinations. Three out of six is an arbitrary number, of course, and I'm not suggesting that such an approach is ideal or even preferable to other combinations. It is, however, a set of combinations that can be analyzed within the data set, as demonstrated in **Figure 1-1**.

For both DSO and inventory turnover, faster is considered better. There is some debate regarding this, but the prevailing mentality in distribution is that firms should try to collect faster and turn inventory faster.

The following exhibit lists all of the three-prong plans ranked from largest positive impact on profit before taxes (PBT) to the smallest. The left side of the exhibit consists of a series of checkmarks identifying which of the three CPVs are incorporated into the specific profit plan.

For each of the 20 plans, three items are reported:

Impact on PBT – the percentage change in profit before taxes generated by firms following this plan.

Resulting PBT – Using three different sample firms (low margin, midsize margin and high margin) as a baseline, this is the actual profit before taxes that would be produced for a firm if statistical relationships held true.

Figure 1-1: Analysis of Profit Plans and the Impact on ROA

	Sales size	Sales growth	GM	Oper. exp.	DSO	Inv. turn	Relative PBT	Resulting PBT Low	Mid	High	# of firms
1			✓	✓	✓		147.5	2.5	6.2	8.7	42
2	✓			✓	✓		122.2	2.2	5.6	7.8	53
3		✓		✓	✓		120.5	2.2	5.5	7.7	42
4		✓		✓		✓	118.8	2.2	5.5	7.7	37
5		✓		✓	✓		65.6	1.7	4.1	5.8	121
6	✓			✓	✓		60.9	1.6	4.0	5.6	113
7	✓	✓			✓		58.7	1.6	4.0	5.6	104
8	✓		✓			✓	57.9	1.6	3.9	5.5	71
9	✓		✓		✓		57.9	1.6	3.9	5.5	79
10	✓	✓	✓				56.1	1.6	3.9	5.5	96
11				✓	✓	✓	50.0	1.5	3.8	5.3	124
12	✓	✓		✓			46.3	1.5	3.7	5.1	158
13		✓	✓		✓		43.5	1.4	3.6	5.0	97
14		✓	✓			✓	40.6	1.4	3.5	4.9	73
15	✓				✓	✓	36.8	1.4	3.4	4.8	96
16	✓	✓				✓	31.3	1.3	3.3	4.6	119
17		✓		✓		✓	31.0	1.3	3.3	4.6	145
18	✓			✓		✓	28.9	1.3	3.2	4.5	154
19		✓			✓	✓	28.8	1.3	3.2	4.5	114
20			✓		✓	✓	3.4	1.0	2.6	3.6	86
All 6	✓	✓	✓	✓	✓	✓	128.6	2.3	5.7	8.0	9

Number of firms using – The total on the exhibit is higher than the actual number of firms in the data set. This is because some firms will fall into more than one category if they are using more than three categories.

Every unique combination of three items, when taken collectively, has a positive impact on profit before taxes. This suggests that if a firm could focus randomly on any three items and perform above the industry norm on those three, the resulting PBT would also be above industry norm.

However, the improvement levels are far from equal. The range of impact runs from 147.5 percent better at the top to 3.4 percent better at the bottom. Also interesting to note, remember that managing all six critical profit values effectively only increased PBT by 128.6 percent. The top four of the "three CPVs at a time" plans were virtually as profitable as the "all six at once" plan.

The table also indicates that the top items are heavily geared toward gross margin and operating expenses. At the other extreme, all seven of the lowest PBT profit plans included inventory turnover.

Figure 1-2: Relationship between Impact of Profit Plans on PBT and Usage by Distributors

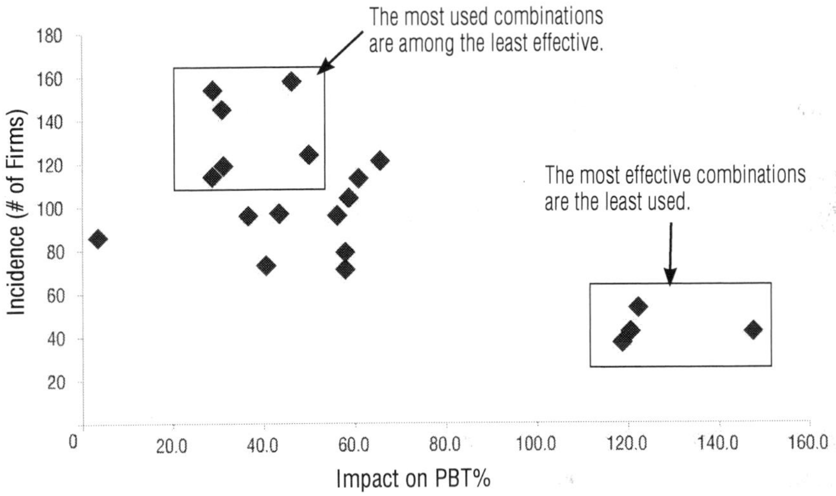

And the combinations with the greatest impact on PBT were the least likely combinations to be used by firms in the study. In fact, the four most profitable plans were the four with the lowest level of usage.

The imbalance between impact on PBT and usage in distribution is obvious, as shown in the scatter diagram in **Figure 1-2**. The four real profit enhancing combinations are resting somewhat forlornly at the lower right-hand corner of the diagram.

Not quite as obvious is the popularity cluster of six plans toward the upper left side of the graph. All six are widely implemented but are in the bottom half of the plans in terms of PBT improvement.

Figure 1-3: Analysis of Profit Plans and the Impact on ROA

	Sales Size	Sales Growth	GM	Oper. Exp.	DSO	Inv. Turn	Relative ROA	Resulting ROA	# of firms
1			✓	✓	✓		156.4	20.5	42
2			✓	✓		✓	131.5	18.5	37
3		✓	✓	✓			117.6	17.4	42
4	✓		✓	✓			83.1	14.7	53
5		✓		✓	✓		69.9	13.6	121
6	✓			✓	✓		66.7	13.3	113
7	✓	✓			✓		64.3	13.1	104
8				✓	✓	✓	63.6	13.1	124
9	✓				✓	✓	56.6	12.5	96
10	✓		✓			✓	56.2	12.5	71
11	✓	✓		✓			54.8	12.4	158
12	✓			✓	✓		51.5	12.1	79
13	✓	✓	✓				51.0	12.1	96
14	✓	✓				✓	50.6	12.0	119
15		✓	✓			✓	50.6	12.0	73
16	✓			✓		✓	46.1	11.7	145
17	✓			✓		✓	40.7	11.3	154
18		✓			✓	✓	39.3	11.1	114
19		✓	✓		✓		37.7	11.0	97
20		✓			✓	✓	10.6	8.8	86
All 6	✓	✓	✓	✓	✓	✓	182.5	22.6	9

Clearly there is a profit implication if more firms are following approaches that have a smaller impact on profit before taxes, but it also should create enthusiasm and opportunity to drive PBT levels higher by shifting that focus.

We can examine the impact on return on assets of each of these plans as well. While profit before taxes and return on assets are highly correlated, there are some notable differences where the plans fall on the chart. Because ROA incorporates an investment component in the measure, days sales outstanding and inventory turnover rise somewhat in the rankings at both the top and bottom of the list.

Even so, the top four combinations in the first table are also the top four combinations in the second, albeit in a slightly different order. They also

Chapter 1 - Choose the Right Variables to Measure

continue to be the four that are employed by the lowest number of firms in the research.

The four plans that are clearly the leader in improving profit in both measures are:

- Gross margin, operating expenses and DSO;
- Gross margin, operating expenses and inventory turnover;
- Gross margin, operating expenses and sales growth;
- Gross margin, operating expenses and sales size.

The redundancy of gross margin and operating expenses is obvious, so the path to profit, at least empirically, goes through the internal operations aspects of managing margins and expenses.

On the lower end of impact, there is one plan that has almost no impact on profitability – gross margin, inventory turnover and DSO. Even so, this plan is used extensively by firms in this research.

The combination of gross margin with two investment factors as the lowest performing – yet widely used – combination may be a statistical fluke. However, it conjures up memories of outmoded management metrics, such as gross margin return on investment, which try to tie margin and inventory together in a return on investment format.

The use of metrics such as gross margin return on investment to evaluate items or gross margin per dollar of accounts receivable to evaluate customers continues to doom firms to employing anachronistic concepts in a technological age. And it appears to lead directly to lower profit performance.

More on Gross Margin and Operating Expenses

Both tables suggest that the most successful firms combine strong gross margin percentage with strong operating expense percentage. After that, it didn't really make any real difference what additional strategy was employed. The problem in improving profitability was that very few firms could put together any of the most profitable combinations.

The reason behind this is that gross margin percentage and operating expense percentage are the only two independent variables in this analysis that are highly correlated. That means that firms with a high gross margin percentage will almost always have a high operating expense percentage, as well. Combining a high gross margin percentage with a low operating expense percentage is incredibly difficult.

However, any firm that is able to break the gross margin/operating expense relationship should be able to generate exceptional profits. Let's look at this relationship a little more closely.

Firms able to move beyond the third quintile on both gross margin and operating expenses do not perform inordinately well on either variable. By definition, they were better than 60 percent of the firms in the research project. What set them apart was the ability to outperform 60 percent of the firms on both metrics at the same time.

Only 35 out of the 885 firms – slightly less than 4 percent – were able to reach this level of performance. But the reward for doing so was huge. This group of firms collectively produced a return on assets that was 189.7 percent higher than norm. In actual ROA terms: They had an ROA of 15.2 percent versus the 8 percent base set of results.

Given that both gross margin and operating expenses impact profit before taxes and not asset investment, the PBT difference was even great. Firms in the superior group had PBT that was 226.3 percent higher than norm.

Any standard that can only be reached by 4 percent of firms is probably overly aggressive in character, but by focusing some efforts to improve these two CPVs can have impressive results. A firm need only excel in one of them, while merely improving the other metric to "above typical."

Implications for Action

Research projects can do no more than suggest areas to consider. Ultimately management must make the decision on the direction to take.

The research may suggest that operational excellence and cost control are statistically more likely to generate higher profit, but if a firm has no appetite to implement those changes, the research is merely an academic exercise.

Having said that, if the four top profit-generating plans all combine gross margin and operating expenses together, then firms ignore that reality at their own peril.

All that can be done here is to highlight the potential and how choosing the right metrics can have impressive results.

Action Steps: Critical Profit Variables

- Understand that a small number of performance factors drive profit, and when these critical profit variables (CPVs) are combined properly, profit surges ahead. The vast majority of distributors don't manage based on this simple and powerful concept.

- Don't boil the ocean. Focus on two of six critical profit variables – gross margin percentage and operating expense margin – to boost profitability.

- Consider the following three management issues to plan the best course of action:

  - The profit impact of a specific action

  - The difficulty of implementing that action

  - The responsiveness of the firm to taking that action

About the Author

Dr. Albert D. Bates is the founder and chairman of Profit Planning Group, a provider of financial benchmarking data and services in distribution. Some of the concepts in this chapter also appeared in other works by Bates, including his latest work, The Real Profit Drivers: Managing the CPVs.

Chapter 2

Profit Analytics:
Develop and Use Profit Analytics

Randy MacLean, WayPoint Analytics

Analytics-driven operations can deliver staggering profit gains, but it takes a visionary leader to direct any kind of data initiative – a leader who won't accept a company's limited analytical expertise and will instead tackle this need head on. In this chapter, distributors will learn how to shift from a revenue-share mindset to a profit-share mindset by zeroing in on three key metrics – gross profit, cost to serve and net before compensation. It also outlines how the concepts of line-item profit analytics and quantum costing can create an effective analytics environment.

The pursuit of profit gains and the optimization of profit production have been business priorities since the dawn of commerce. Advances in computing technology and the pressures of an increasingly competitive marketplace have brought the need for profit analytics to a fever pitch.

Just a few years ago, pioneering executives used what were then state-of-the-art spreadsheets, with hundreds of calculations that delivered insights into the profit-driving elements of their business.

With the advent of today's line-item profit analytics (LIPA) systems, companies can simultaneously use hundreds, thousands or even tens of thousands of factors – through hundreds of millions or billions of calculations – to compute profitability on every line of every invoice.

This has contributed enormously to the science of profit dynamics and produced stunning new insights into the way activities and practices contribute to, or detract from, the bottom line. As with every science that has come before, much of what we thought we knew (also known as conventional wisdom) has been disproved by the profit data. It requires us to rethink the way things are done.

Many distribution company executives and owners have gone back to basics and rebuilt the core of their culture and operations. In a world where a double-digit profit gain would make a hero of any company president, the new profit analytics-driven operations are delivering 100 percent, 300 percent and 600 percent profit gains.

How We Got Here

Throughout recorded history, smart managers have invented and employed rule-of-thumb guidelines, which have aided and hastened decision-making by suggesting a "good" result "most of the time." They have also led to horrible results when they are misapplied or don't provide proper guidance.

Almost every senior manager, at one time or another, has gone through the exercise of trying to estimate the average size of a "good" order or the average margin required for a sale to be "profitable." Statistically, this can be a useful tool when trying to estimate a wide range of possible future results, but it's terrible when trying to evaluate an individual order.

For example, the current average height of a man in the United States is 5 feet, 10 ½ inches. If you're trying to aim a surveillance camera at a doorway, this will give you a very good central aiming point to accommodate most of the people that may walk through the door. But if you are trying to predict the height of the next man that walks through the door, you will be wrong in almost every case. Your prediction can be true only if the next person that walks through the door happens to exactly match the average.

In the same way, a particular order will achieve your average profit only if it exactly matches your average revenue, average margin and average cost structure.

This weird zeal for averages has led to very poor performance levels in the distribution business, as companies' management direction and training drives their whole organization's performance toward average. When some portion of the company inevitably underperforms, it directly results in a below-average performance for the company.

As our understanding of profit dynamics has grown, the companies led by the best executives have moved to new practices that are driven by – and directly contribute to – profit generation. Although the large companies have the resources to employ analytical talent, it is smaller companies directly controlled by visionary owners that have been first to adopt the new thinking to a competitive advantage. For the most part, mid-range companies have the most trouble jumping to hyperspeed because they lack analytical expertise and have several groups of people in the decision-making loop.

The Competitive Gap

A fundamental of market dynamics is that a defined market produces a finite profit opportunity. The players who service the market each take a share of the market's profit pool. The concept of market share is reasonably well known but is most commonly thought of as related to revenue. More beneficially, it can be used to strategize profit production, considering the bulk of the profit pool is made up of customers that are very efficient in their operations and represents greater-than-average profit opportunities.

Almost every market has a dominant seller that takes more than 50 percent of the available profit in the market space. The remaining sellers divide up the rest, and the gap between the big dog and the rest can be very difficult to cross. Crossing the divide means taking the leadership position in profit production and relegating the former leader to an average player status.

If the dominant player doesn't have a solid grasp on how profits are actually generated – and most companies don't – there is a high risk of losing leadership to another player that does and that acts on this knowledge.

Companies that shift from a "revenue share" stance to the "profit share" stance have a good shot at taking the leadership position, regardless of size.

In the future, nearly every company will be data-driven, and that will lock most players into their place in the existing order. Some significant new competitive advantage will be required to shake up the rankings. Right now, however, new understanding of profit dynamics gives everyone the opportunity to be first and to take that profit leadership spot.

Where Did We Go Wrong?

Most executives don't know how a distribution company really makes money. Until I spent time in the analytics, I didn't either. Almost all of us were drawn by the seductive allure of profit averages, and this has led us very far astray.

A distribution business is made up of money-making and money-losing sales, and the bottom line is nothing more than the net of the profits made on the former minus the losses taken on the latter. This is the first critical component of the true understanding of the profit dynamics in wholesale distribution.

The concept of an average sale generating an average profit has resulted in the implicit conclusion that every sale we win will make some "average" profit contribution to the bottom line. This is wrong.

In reality, each sale has a particular gross profit (GP) number and carries its own specific cost based on the amount and cost of infrastructure needed to support it. We refer to this cost as cost to serve (CTS). Where CTS exceeds GP, the sale contributes a loss to the bottom line. This is the second critical component of the true understanding of profit dynamics.

These two core concepts are critical elements to rebuilding our under-standing of how companies make money, and they directly suggest the things that can be done to generate profits in a new and reliable way.

Whale Curves

For a complete understanding of how important this is, I need to intro-duce scale to this line of thinking.

In most distribution companies, only 30 percent to 35 percent of sales are profitable. That narrow band of sales produces a profit of an as-tounding 4 to 5 times the company's eventual bottom line. In other words, one-third of your sales produce profits at least four times your bottom line – and 80 percent of the profits made on those sales is lost to dysfunctional sales that contribute losses.

This is why the profit potential is so enormous – all the profit needed to double or triple the bottom line already exists in the sales you're already servicing. If you can quickly get a handle on the dysfunctional sales, more of your already-existing profit can be retained. It's also why the profit gains are immediate – not hoped-for in some distant future.

A helpful way to visualize this interaction of money-making and money-losing orders is with the use of a "whale curve." This is a graph of cumulative profit with individual results ranked from most positive to most negative. It starts with a blank chart and puts the most profit-able item on first, then stacks the second most profitable item on top of it, continuing until the ranking gets to the point of having listed all of the profitable elements. It continues by charting the losses from the least negative to most at the right-hand end.

In a single chart, the most critical elements in thinking about profit production are conveyed. It also reveals an important new metric, peak internal profit (PIP), which indicates how much profit was made on only the profitable sales.

In **Figure 2-1,** a company generates $5.3 million of sold, delivered and collected profits on about 25 percent of its sales, represented on the left side of the curve. It then loses about $4 million of that to money-losing sales on the worst 35 percent, as seen on the right side of the curve. This leaves the company with about $1.3 million in net profit. Without analytics, the company executive is blind to the actual profit generation within the business and is doing absolutely nothing to capture it.

Figure 2-1: Whale Curve

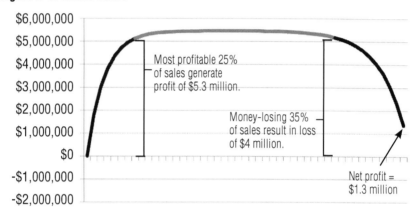

Whale curve charts can be made for sales, invoice lines, product lines or customers and products. All are useful in understanding the entities that contribute to or detract from profitability.

The curve of invoice lines is special and gives us the actual optimum peak internal profit. The others will all deliver lower peak internal profit numbers as each of the elements can potentially be made up of money-making and money-losing invoice lines, which net out to a lower number. This doesn't diminish the utility of these other curves but guides us to use the invoice-line curve when evaluating profit potential.

Profit Dynamics of an Order

Taking a closer look at the profit dynamics of an individual order facilitates the translation of this new knowledge into profit-driving action. There are three metrics associated with an invoice that are critical to profit production.

The first is gross profit, the dollar amount left after cost of goods sold is deducted from revenue. Gross profit is a function of the total sale amount and the margin rate. It is, in fact, the operating budget for servicing the order. The service costs of the order must be less than the gross profit for the sale to be profitable.

The second is the operating expense total for the order, or cost to serve, which consists of all the normal operating expenses of the business, excepting pay for the customer facing sales reps. CTS is almost exclusively a function of the logistics costs and company overhead associated with the particular order.

The third is a metric called net before compensation, which is gross profit less cost to serve. This is the most important of the three metrics, replacing gross margin in the vernacular and day-to-day operations of companies driving toward profit generation.

On a larger scale, gross profit is a function of volume and pricing. Cost to serve is driven largely by transaction counts: the number of invoices, shipments, orders and warehouse picks. Net before compensation is a metric that takes all of this into account and is the one metric everyone should be working to drive upward.

About Gross Margin

If there's one thing that has contributed more than anything else to the destruction of profitability in distribution, it's gross margin. The widespread misuse and abuse of the gross margin metric has completely disconnected most sales forces in most organizations from profit production.

Gross margin is gross profit divided into revenue, and the only useful purpose for it is as an indicator of the magnitude of markup as applied to the cost of the product. Because it does not account for cost to serve, it is completely disconnected from profit and is useless as a predictor of profitability.

Mathematically, it's easy to see the problem. For most sales, achievable gross margin falls within a narrow range (15 percent to 35 percent). Cost to serve can vary from 0 percent all the way up to 100 percent – or more. A sale with a 60 percent cost to serve is not going to be fixed by getting the margin up to 35 percent. Because of this, cost to serve has a far greater impact on – and is a far better predictor of – a given sale's profitability.

In organizations where gross margin is a central management tool, profit production is almost accidental. Whatever bottom line is achieved is largely the result of the random combination of profitable and unprofitable orders, neither of which is strongly influenced by gross margin. The companies moving most quickly into a high-profit-rate future have switched to net before compensation as a ruling factor in evaluating the profit potential of orders.

The Arrival of Granular Profit Analytics

The new technology that's changing everything is line-item profit analytics. LIPA takes dozens (or hundreds or thousands) of individual costs and marries them to thousands of individual and intersecting transaction pools, using hundreds of millions of computations to calculate the complete cost structure and profit of every line on every invoice.

New LIPA systems take business costing to the ultimate level – well beyond the ability of human brains to visualize and validate. Unseen and unexpected interactions between various cost structures and related transaction pools have produced surprising results. This has introduced important – and sometimes, counterintuitive – new thinking into our understanding of how profit is generated.

For instance, products that tend to be purchased on multi-line orders, which may be shipped directly from the manufacturer, will have much greater profit rates – even when they have much lower margins.

In a line-item profit analytics system, there will be a complete and detailed P&L for every invoice line. The system will know the revenue, the cost of goods sold, the cost to serve, the net before compensation, the sales pay and the net profit on every line. It will also reflect the complex interactions between customer order tendencies, company logistical elements and product-to-product relationships.

These all impact profitability in a real way but are far too complex to model in spreadsheets (or in your head).

Since line-item profit analytics information can be aggregated up to any level, there will be a complete profit picture for: every invoice, every customer, every product, every product line, every branch, every territory, etc.

Quantum Costing

Line-item profit analytics is based on a new costing methodology called quantum costing. Most executives will be aware of the costing technique known as activity-based costing (ABC), invented in the late 1980s by Dr. Robert Kaplan at Harvard University. ABC was originally designed to solve the costing challenges of manufacturing companies and is probably one of the best methodologies available to manufacturers. It relies on time measurements as a surrogate for many of the cost structures encountered in manufacturing, which tend to be a reasonably good analog for the costs that are actually involved.

However, activity-based costing is not very well suited for use in a distribution environment, where a bottom-up methodology like ABC requires administratively intense maintenance and where activity-to-cost correlation is poor.

Quantum costing was designed specifically for the distribution industry, and its top-down methodology delivers much more accurate results, requiring much higher computational horsepower for a much lower administrative overhead.

Quantum costing isolates individual logistical element costs and marries them to appropriate individual transaction pools. The overlapping intersection of these transaction pools frequently reveals unseen and unexpected correlations inherent in the business itself.

The most sophisticated line-item profit analytics systems tie these results back to each element of the company's infrastructure (e.g., branches, territories, sales reps, product lines, delivery routes, etc.) and to customer and market demographics (e.g., industry, size, geography, headcount, etc.). They can provide startling insights and accurate guidance into a company's best profit potential.

Because time and resources are finite, this gives companies the ability to shift focus away from activities and accounts that drive losses and toward areas where profits can be most quickly and easily obtained. This allows companies to develop niches, pursue opportunities and capitalize on emerging market opportunities. When they have these insights first, companies can dominate the profit pool in each of their market areas.

Business Intelligence

Business intelligence is a marketing term for add-on reporting systems with a core purpose to add reports and graphs to software that lacks them. BI systems take information you already have and give you new ways to report on it or visualize it.

Unlike BI, line-item profit analytics systems need to compute underlying cost and profit data, and then produce profit-specific reporting on that new data.

Business intelligence is an excellent tool for managers to further access and evaluate information in existing systems, but it is not capable of providing the profit guidance of line-item profit analytics systems. Conversely, LIPA systems are so profit-specific they can't display other information.

The two kinds of systems frequently coexist, but neither is a replacement of the other.

Critical Metrics

There are metrics and methodologies you can implement to get a good, solid start on your own data- and analytics-driven environment. Before beginning, let me review and define the terms I'll be using:

- **Revenue (Rev)**: Net revenue or amount billed
- **Cost of goods sold (CoGS)**: Cost of products and services delivered to customer
- **Gross profit (GP)**: Dollar amount of raw profits when CoGS is deducted from Rev (GP = Rev - CoGS)
- **Gross margin (GM%)**: Percentage of Rev that GP represents (GM% = GP ÷ Rev x 100)
- **Cost to serve (CTS)**: Total operating expenses, excluding pay for customer-facing sales reps
- **CTS rate (CTS%)**: Percentage of Rev that CTS represents (CTS% = CTS ÷ Rev x 100)
- **Net before (sales) compensation (NBC)**: Profit generated after deducting operating expenses but not sales compensation costs from GP (NBC = GP - CTS)
- **NBC rate (NBC%)**: Percentage of Rev that NBC represents (NBC ÷ Rev)
- **Net before taxes (NBT)**: "Bottom line" profit on a standard P&L (GP - CTS - sales compensation)
- **NBT rate (NBT%)**: Percentage of Rev that NBT represents (NBT ÷ Rev)
- **Peak internal profit (PIP)**: Total of all realized positive profits - the peak of the profit "whale curve"

Restructuring Your Profit & Loss Statement

The first thing to do in your own analytical environment is develop a P&L structure suited for profitability analytics. To do this, it's a good idea to create at least one customized P&L report in your existing ERP system.

For maximum utility, consolidate all of the detailed subaccounts up to the level of your main logistics cost drivers. Your report may look something like this:

Figure 2-2: Profit & Loss Report

Revenue	$39,655,812	
Cost of Goods	$30,860,830	
GP	$8,794,982	22.2%
Order Entry	$267,765	
Warehouse	$1,492,732	
Delivery	$992,897	
G & A	$1,751,544	
CTS	$4,504,938	11.4%
NBC	$4,290,044	10.8%
Sales Comp	$2,346,117	
NBT	$1,943,927	4.9%

This structure is well-suited to profit analysis for the following reasons.

Revenue

An important concept in profit analytics is that revenue is irrelevant. The numbers are useful for bragging rights at cocktail parties and association events but are so far removed from actual profit production that they are completely useless for evaluating the real success of a company.

Gross Profit

The first important number is gross profit, which should be considered the operating budget for the company, branch or sale. Gross profit can be increased by raising the amount of product on the sale or by increasing the margin used to set the sale price. It can also be increased on a per-transaction basis by encouraging orders, sales or deliveries to be combined. This creates an environment where the unit gross profit is much more likely to exceed the cost to serve, producing a larger profit.

Cost to Serve

The next important element is cost to serve, which is largely driven by transaction counts. Increasing numbers of orders, picks, invoices or deliveries drives up the scale of the infrastructure needed to service a given gross profit envelope.

The fastest way to manage cost to serve is to combine orders, which in turn reduces the number of picks and deliveries, lowering infrastructure and cost requirements. Policy solutions – such as order processing fees, small order charges, delivery charges and policies adding conditions to "free" delivery – can quickly reduce infrastructure requirements and open the door to infrastructure reductions that will translate directly into cost savings.

In the absence of infrastructure and personnel reductions, these requirement reductions also translate into faster and better service for profit-generating accounts and can spur growth that no longer drives the need for more infrastructure. Increases in gross profit that don't increase cost to serve contribute directly to the bottom line.

Cost to serve can also be improved by eliminating infrastructure costs for certain classes of sales. In the case of small accounts or small orders, eliminating sales commissions, free delivery and trade credit can produce significant reductions in the company's infrastructure costs, changing the profit picture in a big way.

This is the path to developing a low-cost service model geared to profitably handle small orders.

Net Before Compensation

The net before compensation metric is, perhaps, the most important of all. Unlike gross margin and other commonly used metrics, it encompasses both gross profit generation and infrastructure cost utilization to produce a useful end result that can be managed in different ways.

Net before compensation is improved by increasing volume, increasing margin, reducing product costs, or reducing or eliminating any number of infrastructure costs. All of these changes are beneficial to the company's bottom line, and most of them can be put in the direct control of the sales force. For this reason, many companies are moving to a much simpler NBC-driven sales compensation program, rewarding sales reps where any profit-related dynamic can be driven for NBC improvement.

Using these simple and readily available metrics in your own organization will get you started on the path to a profit- and data-driven culture.

How LIPA Changes Everything

Companies that have LIPA systems can use what the systems reveal about how profit is made and lost in ways that extend profit-driven decision-making into almost every aspect of the company's operations.

Sales Compensation

Profit metrics, particularly NBC, ensures the company pays only for – and the sales force is rewarded only for – money-making transactions. For decades, this has been the Holy Grail of sales compensation, and companies have expended enormous amounts of time and money trying to find surrogate measures that would deliver this result.

Practices like eliminating commissions below a certain gross margin or gross profit floor, having "house" accounts or implementing "load factors" have all had the intent of restricting sales incentives only to profitable orders. These surrogates for profitability have rarely been accurate and have created a fair amount of dysfunction in the sales and sales compensation process.

All of these can be eliminated and companies can move directly to pay-for-profit by adopting NBC-based incentives.

Customer Segmentation

Customer segmentation can be a powerful tool in identifying the best kind of customers, and LIPA data can identify the accounts most likely to deliver the best profits. Naturally, it's also useful to identify customers most likely to produce losses.

Unfortunately, segmentation has most commonly been based on customer attributes that are easily seen but are not correlated to profitability in any way. These things include industry, customer size, geography and others that have no correlation to the value – or profitability – of the customer.

In our segmentation work, we use the four-quadrant approach developed by Dr. Barry Lawrence at Texas A&M University (see **Figure 2-3**). In this methodology, customer accounts are assigned to four quadrants in a 2 x 2 grid, with each of the cells indicating the profit value of the customer and suggesting the types of activities that should be dedicated to customers in that quadrant.

Figure 2-3: Customer Segmentation

Opportunistic high invoice profit low volume	increase volume convert to core	Core high invoice profit high volume	protect penetrate
Customers: 293	Invoices: 1,974	Customers: 119	Invoices: 15,757
Total GP: $658,154	Avg GP: $333	Total GP: $7,005,998	Avg GP: $445
Total NBC: $317,212	Avg NBC: $161	Total NBC: $3,992,399	Avg NBC: $253
Total Net: $138,084	Avg Net: $70	Total Net: $2,213,464	Avg Net: $140
Marginal low invoice profit low volume	restructure attrition	Service Drain low invoice profit high volume	convert to core reduce expenses
Customers: 586	Invoices: 6,691	Customers: 38	Invoices: 6,263
Total GP: $626,631	Avg GP: $94	Total GP: $659,089	Avg GP: $105
Total NBC: ($562,407)	Avg NBC: ($84)	Total NBC: ($577,643)	Avg NBC: ($92)
Total Net: ($734,133)	Avg Net: ($110)	Total Net: ($793,973)	Avg Net: ($127)

Customers with positive net before compensation are distributed into the top two quadrants; those with negative NBC to the bottom two. The average gross profit production of money-making customers is determined, and customers with less than average gross profit production (either positive or negative) are moved into the left two quadrants. The balance are moved into the right two quadrants.

The absolute value of a particular customer's profit production is compared to the average gross profit production of the money-making accounts only, and this is used to determine whether the account belongs in the left half or the right half of the table.

This segmentation table packs a lot of information into a small space. For each quadrant, there's an indicator of invoice profit and volume, indicators of the appropriate strategic actions for accounts in the group, a count of the number of customers in the group, aggregations of the group's gross profit, NBC and net profit, an invoice count indicating the transaction volume, and per-invoice averages of gross profit, NBC and net profit.

The quadrants are also suggestive of the kinds of customers that inhabit them:

Core: These accounts drive the company's current profit picture. The loss of any of these accounts would affect the company materially, so to protect and preserve them, the company should prioritize its attention and resources to service these accounts very well. They should also be in the hands of the most capable sales reps, those more likely to drive larger volumes by finding new opportunities to deliver more product into them.

Opportunity: These accounts are profitable but drive lower profit levels due to their smaller size. In this quadrant, there are two important subgroups, both of which can contribute to the company's growth. The first subgroup is new and emerging accounts that are growing at high rates inherent in their own operations. The second subgroup consists of large players that are using your company as second source. Investing time and effort to win these accounts over will put them straight into the core group, contributing significantly to the company's bottom line.

Marginal: These accounts are small-volume, money-losing accounts, working on a dysfunctional service model where the CTS is greater than the gross profit production. They are an artifact of the company's history, left over from the days when the company was small and better suited to work only with small accounts. The activity of servicing these accounts has been propagated by the erroneous idea that every sale somehow contributes to the bottom line. Creating a differentiated low-cost to serve service model can immediately move most of these accounts into the money-making opportunity group.

Service Drain: The remaining accounts are large-volume, money-losing accounts that are always a significant drain on the company's profits. They make up the rapid down slope on the right-hand side of the whale curve. Accounts in this group are large-volume companies that are either extremely disorganized in their procurement process or have transferred a significant portion of their distribution costs over to your business. In the latter case, they are, effectively, large groups of marginal accounts operated under the umbrella of a single headquarters (e.g., big-box stores).

Intelligent Pricing

For some time, companies have realized that different customer segments need different pricing models. Companies that have invested in intelligent pricing programs have seen permanent profit gains.

When line-item profit analytics data is integrated, intelligent pricing goes into hyperdrive. The company can ensure that gross profit production is adequate to cover cost structures on a much larger range of sales.

Since the market is inherently efficient, price levels always settle to points necessary for producing a small profit. Since LIPA data will give reasonably accurate cost data, it can be a very good predictor of likely price points in the absence of current market data.

Market Demographics

Combining customer demographic information with LIPA data can be extremely useful in prioritizing sales and marketing efforts, investing resources in market segments most likely to generate extraordinary profits.

Companies also frequently take this practice to the next level by obtaining market data that can help them target high-profit account types that exist in markets where they have low market share.

Policy and Operations

LIPA data can also guide and prioritize internal initiatives. Restructuring warehousing and delivery operations based on profit opportunity or CTS challenges can produce big dividends.

Ensuring these initiatives, and the cost envelopes associated with them, are profit data-driven is important to optimizing company results.

Implications for Action

The market is shifting rapidly in the direction of analytics-driven decision-making. This presents a huge opportunity for companies to drive much greater levels of profit out of the business that they already have and visibility into profit opportunities other companies don't see.

Executives that seize the opportunity first will drive profit rates up by 100 percent, 300 percent, 500 percent or more. Results will be well beyond historical records or expectations, and these companies will achieve substantial and permanent leadership positions in their markets, geographies and associations.

Companies that are slow to adopt the new methods will never close the gap the new leaders establish. Make sure your company is a member of the first group.

Action Steps: Profit Analytics

- Commit to becoming a profit data-driven company. Communicate and reward this down through the ranks.
  Educate every person in the company on the real math of profit generation. Make sure this is integrated into their decision-making, so the company is less likely to produce money-losing orders.

- Obtain and implement a LIPA system to get good, accurate profit visibility at every level of the company sales operations.

- End practices, such as gross margin management, that lead to dysfunctional sales. Replace these with better, profit-driven alternatives.

About the Author

Randy MacLean is president of WayPoint Analytics, a profitability service provider for distribution companies. He can be reached at rmaclean@waypoint-analytics.com, or visit his website at www.randymaclean.com.

Chapter 3

Market Analytics:
Mine the Gap: World-Class Market Analytics

Thomas P. Gale, MDM Analytics

Market analytics is the combined effort to analyze data about customers, geographic markets and the competitive dynamics that impact the markets. Top-performing companies use market analytics to gain better visibility into addressable market size, market share and wallet share at target accounts. They deploy a more effective sales and marketing process and make better decisions about growth strategy based on market data analysis. This chapter is a primer on the core elements of market analytics – segmentation, profiling and modeling – that can help your company grow faster and be more adaptive than competitors.

How do you rate your sales and marketing organization – against direct competitors, marketing group peers or best-in-class companies and industries you admire? Do any of the following ring true?

- **Data-free discussion**: We repeatedly talk about market share and whether we are getting as much as we can out of specific accounts in sales, marketing and management meetings, often with no actionable result.
- **Shotgun selling**: Our salespeople have too many accounts and a diluted focus that too often causes a presentation spray-paint approach. They also spend too much time selling to existing customers without a clear agenda.
- **Sales silos**: Our salespeople hold knowledge about their customers close to the vest; we don't have a CRM system or

an effective way to extract and share customer data across the organization.

- **Daily fire drill**: We should get more intentional about marketing but are just able to keep up in this strong business cycle.

All of the above describe the sales and marketing Groundhog Day syndrome many wholesale distribution companies wrestle with. A small percentage of companies have created a very different storyline, one that shares some or all of the following characteristics and defines market analytics capability:

- **Market profile**: We estimate the size and makeup of our realistic addressable market and use that to create business plans, forecast, set goals and measure sales and marketing efforts. We evaluate new territory and customer acquisition opportunity by profiling the "market DNA" – the market potential for our unique product portfolio.
- **Market share**: We estimate our penetration into specific territories by sales rep, product category and customer segment. We use this data to build realistic sales quotas, target marketing and sales resources, and to create joint-marketing efforts with suppliers.
- **Wallet share**: We profile individual account potential in our existing customers and identify patterns to target high-growth-potential accounts to increase our share.
- **Target account prospecting**: We benchmark our "sweet-spot" customers across the segments we serve and use that to estimate total market potential and target similar companies not currently served.

The difference between these two scenarios illustrates a very real competitive gap, one that is widening quickly. But there's a way to recover from Groundhog Day syndrome: Build a market analytics capability and culture focused on market intelligence. Many companies say they are customer centric, but truly customer-centric companies have processes and systems they keep improving by sharing knowledge of individual customers, customer segments and markets throughout the organization. Companies with market analytics capability have better visibility; they can see where to mine the gap.

Market analytics is the final frontier of distribution analytics. Wholesale distributors have continued to build their internal analytics capabilities from a focus in the 1990s on process quality (fill rate, return rate, etc.) to more strategic analytic tools described elsewhere in this book. For that reason, market analytics is a largely untapped area – that invisible gap! – where distributors can create significant competitive advantage. If you don't mine that gap, your competitors will. Some of them already are.

Historically, sales (including outside sales salaries and commission, as well as inside/counter sales wages) is the single largest expense category, most often consuming 20 percent to 30 percent of gross margin dollars, based on benchmarking studies by Profit Planning Group's annual Distributor Profitability Reports across dozens of trade associations. Yet the sales function is typically the least managed and measured aspect of distribution operations. While many chicken-and-egg arguments can be made for top-line revenue or sales as being the most critical measurement of all, I'd argue this is precisely the problem.

As we approach the mid-mark of this decade, today's market environment is characterized by an unprecedented acceleration of technology in turbulent markets, with new, disruptive and alternate supply sources (e.g., AmazonSupply.com, Alibaba, national catalog and big-box stores). Traditional sales-driven distribution models no longer hold the edge; distributors need to shift to a focus on market strategy based on analytics to differentiate and compete effectively.

The golden sales egg has lost some of its luster as companies with traditional distribution financial models strive to increase profitability and efficiency. Top-performing companies use market analytics to build a more efficient and effective sales and marketing strategy, one that identifies and targets growth.

Foundations of Market Analytics

Market intelligence is a key differentiator today; companies with better visibility into their markets gain critical perspective that allows them to be proactive, rather than reactive, to competitive threats such as price wars, digital marketing channels or other forces outside their control. Instead, a focus on their core differentiating products and service portfolio allows them to maintain sustainable margins and deepen their value to customers. They intentionally target the heart of the markets that yield the highest return on their invested resources.

Market analytics can be defined as the combined skill sets that yield a market intelligence capability within a company. Like a muscle, it can be trained and developed in an organization. A deep market intelligence capability can be divided into three core areas:

- Competitive analysis
- Market analysis
- Customer behavior analysis

Competitive Analysis

Every company operates in a unique market space, one that is defined by a broad range of environmental conditions, among them:

- Macroeconomic and political trends
- New market and regulatory realities
- Shifting customer requirements
- Customer and product lifecycles
- Core, tangential and emerging competitors

Many executive teams share the ongoing responsibility to scan and evaluate these forces to evaluate potential threats and opportunity for the business. It is a critical top-level management skill to process these inputs, then adjust company strategy to either leverage or defend against these constant shifts.

Most wholesale distribution companies have a process for competitive assessment, even if it is an informal one. They attend association and marketing group meetings, subscribe to information services such as Modern Distribution Management, read trade publications and industry trend reports, and attend webinars. Fewer companies have developed process and skill sets around market and customer assessment or assigned job descriptions defining specific roles for market analytics.

Market Analysis

Within the broader strategic competitive and environmental factors above, high-performing companies track key data about market sectors, market size and estimated market share. The foundation for market assessment is segmentation. To be clear, segmentation is not an end in itself. It is a critical step to classify data for analysis. The only way to categorize and identify patterns across diverse product categories, customer segments and geographic territories is through a systematic and standardized classification process that can be as simple or as complex as the desired insight dictates.

Figure 3-1: Market Segmentation Diagram

Total Market				
Industrial	**Non-Industrial**	**Contractor**	**Dealer/Retailer**	**End-User**
•OEM Components •MRO Supplies •Capital Equipment •Service Consumers	•Institutions •Government •Commercial	•Construction •Repair and specialty service	•Store	

Many companies perform fairly deep levels of segmentation internally to measure financial or operational performance and spot trends via reporting from their ERP system. Fewer companies fully tap into their transactional and customer data to perform a more in-depth assessment of their markets and customers.

Market Share & Wallet Share

Building a foundation of knowledge around markets, competitive landscape and customer behavior can help you track your market share overall and wallet share at individual customers. How well are you penetrating the markets you serve? What's the true opportunity for the specific product lines you sell? Distributors have typically built successful companies by serving a relatively small group of customer segments very well with a tailored portfolio of products and services.

Many companies don't try to determine an addressable market size because they feel they can't get an "accurate" estimate. So there is a widening competitive gap between companies still guessing (or not even trying to guess) market size and segmentation and those that have built directional models with benchmarks to profile demand by sales territory, product category and customer segments. The best product marketers work hard to find a meaningful way to determine market share – to reliably benchmark how much upside potential there is for a given territory, product line or customer segment. This valuable market intelligence allows a company to dedicate precious resources into the areas of greatest return and profitability. It defines winners in highly competitive industries.

Once you understand the opportunity at the market level, your ERP system has a wealth of historical sales data to model growth opportunity at specific accounts as well as prospects. You just need to organize it and analyze it. A first step is to segment customers by end-market, either with internal codes or using standard industry classification codes.

Then build a best-in-class model by segment as a benchmark to measure relative share in other similar accounts. It's a basic demand-profiling tool, but better than nothing at all. Don't wait for the tool to be perfect; you can always refine your market profiler as you use it and better understand your markets.

Companies that have embraced these best practices and track market and wallet share have seen a consistent 5 percent to 10 percent increase in year-to-year top-line revenue growth. They set meaningful goals. And they increase their value in the most profitable customer segments, where they have identified growth opportunity.

Market Profiling

Meaningful analytics require a consistent methodology for organizing data into logical groupings. The primary building blocks for market analytics are by territory, customer segment and product category. These three primary variables form the basis for any type of market analytics project. Much finer segmentations can be applied, such as filtering by company revenue, employee size or other attributes specific to certain end markets, such as factors that may impact purchase and product consumption patterns. Let's look at a few specific examples of how segmentation is applied to profiling markets.

Useful market segmentation starts with a definition of the unique customer base within a defined territory. The North American Industry Classification System (NAICS), which has now replaced Standard Industrial Classification (SIC) codes, is the universal reference in North America for building logical segments. (See the reference website for this book for more information.) Typically, a customer list append is sourced through a third-party database service, such as Dun & Bradstreet or Hoovers. In addition to an industry code and description, other firmographic information is retrieved, as well, such as number of employees and estimated annual revenues. These data points contribute to customer profiling and analysis.

Figure 3-2: Market Profile by Industry Sector

2-digit NAICS	Description	Demand for Safety PPE
31-33	Manufacturing	$116,120,668
23	Construction	$83,738,823
21	Mining, Quarrying, and Oil & Gas Extraction	$2,485,955
92	Institutional	$289,498
22	Utilities	$2,130,569

Figure 3-2 is an example of a market profile for safety personal protective equipment, or PPE, products in Illinois. An estimate for the total market size for Illinois has been determined by a third-party market data resource, in this case MDM Analytics. There are many resources and methodologies to build market size estimates, some of which are outlined later in this chapter and other parts of this book.

In this example, end markets are profiled by 2-digit NAICS codes into major industry segments. This gives a bird's eye view of the market demand for each industry segment, broken out by product group. This segmentation ranks industries by annual demand for this product; it also indicates the relative size of opportunity within each segment.

Within each of these high-level industry sectors, there are more detailed segment definitions. For example, within Manufacturing, Motor Vehicle Transmission and Power Train Parts Manufacturing is a discrete industry segment, defined at the 6-digit NAICS code level (NAICS 336350). Categorizing a company's customer list at the 6-digit NAICS code level is the most-used baseline classification for analysis. It's possible to aggregate these sub-segments into higher groupings, depending on the goal of a particular analytic project.

Figure 3-3: Market Profile by Metro Area

Metropolitan Statistical Area (MSA)	Demand for Safety PPE
Chicago-Joliet-Naperville, IL-IN-WI	$150,991,407
St. Louis, MO-IL	$11,691,355
Peoria, IL	$6,951,582
Rockford, IL	$5,258,348
Ottawa-Streator, IL	$4,223,906
Decatur, IL	$3,192,203
Kankakee-Bradley, IL	$2,756,283
Davenport-Moline-Rock Island, IA-IL	$2,724,901
Springfield, IL	$2,589,104

Figure 3-3 illustrates a geographic or territory market-demand segmentation by major metro areas in Illinois, including tangential territory in neighboring states that make up a logical market area. This is a standard classification for metropolitan statistical areas (MSAs). This type of segmentation, again using market size modeling, provides great visibility into the relative opportunity by market.

Even if you don't have a valid method to benchmark market opportunity by product category, it is still possible to compare markets with more macroeconomic indicators. For example, the U.S. Census Bureau maintains a useful QuickFacts website (http://quickfacts.census.gov/qfd/index.html#). It contains a wealth of demographic and business statistical information at the state, county and city levels. You can view and compare data on number of firms, manufacturers' shipments, merchant wholesaler sales, building permits and other indicators that can help you compare with territories where you currently have sales history data.

Figure 3-4: Market Share Profile by Metro Area

Metropolitan Statistical Area (MSA)	Demand for Safety PPE	Sales in Safety PPE	% Share
Chicago-Joliet-Naperville, IL-IN-WI	$150,991,407	$603,964	4%
St. Louis, MO-IL	$11,691,355	$116,913	1%
Peoria, IL	$6,951,582	$1,042,737	15%
Rockford, IL	$5,258,348	$1,289,653	25%
Ottawa-Streator, IL	$4,223,906	$760,303	18%
Decatur, IL	$3,192,203	$856,398	27%
Kankakee-Bradley, IL	$2,756,283	$96,344	3%
Davenport-Moline-Rock Island, IA-IL	$2,724,901	$1,568,796	58%
Springfield, IL	$2,589,104	$310,692	12%

Adding internal transactional data to a market profile produces market share indicators by territory and product category (**Figure 3-4**). Working with key suppliers, distributors can sometimes develop general estimates for specific product market demand. But is it accurate? My answer would be that no model is precisely accurate, but it may be possible to estimate a range of accuracy, such as within 20 percent or 30 percent. For this type of analysis, it's more important to focus on the relative weights the data indicate. In this example, Kankakee and Davenport share a similar market size potential. But this company has dominant market penetration into Davenport (58 percent), and barely scratching Kankakee (3 percent).

Market share analysis can be extended to identify how much of a specific customer's spend your company currently holds. **Figure 3-5** includes sales data (annualized to match demand calculation) to determine wallet share. Together with market share analysis, this is a powerful way to manage sales and marketing resources to prioritize territory development and target account plans.

Figure 3-5: Wallet Share Profile

Company Name	Demand for Safety PPE	Sales in Safety PPE	% Share
Abbott Laboratories	$3,747,967	$1,354,864	36%
Mosaic Global Operations Inc	$2,892,434	$966,458	33%
Enamelers & Japanners Inc	$2,631,265	$236,594	9%
Graphic Packaging Intl Inc	$4,671,794	$3,215,548	69%
Phosphate Resource Ptrs	$1,713,437	$347,849	20%
BP America Inc	$2,294,851	$445,578	19%
ConocoPhillips	$860,569	$46,786	5%
Potash Corp Saskatchewan Sales	$453,930	$287,646	63%
Baxter International Inc	$457,664	$46,486	10%

Benchmarks & Consumption Patterns

Market assessment requires benchmarks to measure market share and wallet share. Developed internally or sourced through third parties, consumption ratios are most effective to benchmark consistently. These are built typically by developing a per-employee consumption model by product and customer segment. The result is a way to measure a total market size or account demand.

Here's an example: MDM Analytics modeling has determined that petroleum refineries (NAICS 324110) use approximately $1,150 of safety PPE products for each employee per year. The state of Kansas has 43 petroleum refineries that employ a total of 3,500 people. Demand for that segment in Kansas is roughly $4 million. Acme Refinery has 150 employees. Their approximate use of safety PPE products is $3,900 annually.

Many product sectors use per-employee ratios at a broad-based level to estimate market potential. For example, annual purchase estimates by electrical contractors (NAICS 238210) for the broad-based category of electrical supplies is typically benchmarked at between $40,000 and $50,000. HVAC contractor (NAICS 23822) annual demand is often profiled slightly higher.

For certain end-markets, other benchmarks can be more effective. These include oil rig counts, machine tool count in a facility, square footage for lighting demand, fleet size and more. Consumption profiling works well in certain types of markets. For example, maintenance, repair, operating and production (MROP) consumable supplies exhibit fairly predictable demand rates based on production levels. More difficult to profile is infrequent or erratic demand, such as capital improvement projects. However, building permit applications or public project requisitions provide ways to track and estimate demand in less predictable markets.

The final component in a market assessment process is the build-out of a database marketing system to continually improve and analyze the data. There are increasing numbers of third-party providers, and more CRM systems are adding features to nurture a master marketing database.

There are two key attributes of a truly effective marketing database system:

- **Data quality keeps improving**. No matter whether sourced internally or externally, large data sets require constant cleansing and updating.
- **Salespeople gather and share front-line data**. Customer data and knowledge is updated and shared. They are revising and validating data at customer accounts and updating the master database so that knowledge is available throughout the organization.

The only way to break the silo mentality of traditional outside sales force models is to reorient the sales process to a collaborative model. Customer knowledge must be transferred and accessible to the team members to effectively break the Groundhog Day syndrome. Don't expect your sales team to embrace this effort; it has to be management driven, with clear goals and a designated champion to move it forward. A strong personality with business analytic skills is a good choice for a champion.

The payoff is significant. A marketing database allows companies to profile and better understand specific territories and customer segments. They can estimate market potential and build forecasts, manage key accounts, define territories, identify prospects and more effectively focus limited sales and marketing resources.

Customer Behavior Analysis

This third level of assessment is a deeper identification of customer behavior patterns and needs by specific customer groupings. The insight gained may be by standard industry classification, but more often will reflect the way in which unique customer groups interact and engage with the distributor, whether in the way they source, purchase or use services.

This type of analysis can provide some of the most significant insight to help a company shift its focus from product-centric to customer-centric, to understand how specific types of customers think about themselves, not how the supplier thinks about them. It often provides the basis for new services and solutions based on data that yield answers to the following critical questions:

- How can we become more embedded in the daily workflow of our customers?
- Instead of making them come to us, how can we bring our products, services and solutions to them as a seamless partner, not a seller?
- How can we help our customers grow their business and become more profitable?

Another type of customer-focused assessment maps specific patterns in purchasing behavior. Recency-frequency-monetary (RFM) analysis is used to analyze customer value and opportunity based on how recently a customer has purchased, how often he buys and how much he spends. Used extensively in retail and professional services industries, it also has value for wholesale distributors. Typically, a matrix is created to identify several segments. The analysis provides the basis for targeting discrete segments with more customized campaigns to drive retention and specific response. (See chapter 5, Customer Profiling for Distributors, for a detailed explanation RFM analysis.)

Mine the Gap!

For most companies, the daily data stream – transaction, customer, market, supplier – is an under-tapped resource. The three foundations of market analytics – competitive, market and customer behavior analysis – provide a powerful three-dimensional visibility into market dynamics that results in better decisions.

Many companies have strengths in one or two of these market analytic dimensions. Few excel across all three; those that do build a competitive position difficult to displace. They are more responsive to changes in customer behavior, anticipate market shifts more quickly and adapt their product and service offerings more specifically to match customer needs. They are difficult to displace from the best accounts, two steps ahead of competitors because they can see farther down the road. These are the real gaps that define sustainable competitive advantage. How can your team leverage market analytics to widen that gap moving forward?

Implications for Action

Building an effective market analytics process is a journey. Where is your firm on its path to building an effective sales and marketing strategy based on a triangulated profiling of your markets? You can jump-start the process by outsourcing specific aspects through third-party benchmarking reports or purchasing expertise to profile your markets and customer segments.

But longer term, this is an internal capability that needs to be planned and nurtured. It often requires a change in the mindset and culture, particularly in those companies with a sales-dominated culture (the majority of distributors).

Market analytics can give you the edge to stay ahead of the competition in today's fast-changing markets. The marketer with the best visibility into the size, shape and opportunity in specific markets tends to win, and win big.

Action Steps: Market Analytics

- Build specific skill sets across the range of qualitative and quantitative metrics to give your company a strong foundation. This is what you need to sustain smarter strategy, to identify growth opportunity, and to target untapped wallet and market share opportunity more effectively and efficiently. Tap data champions that will push the company to act on the data they uncover.

- Prioritize clean, accurate data. Build feedback loops with your sales force so you understand what is happening at customer accounts. Ongoing communication back and forth also allows you to act on unexpected shifts at the customer or market level.

- Set the data free. Improve visibility across your organization – from management to the front lines – so that you can act more quickly on the market intelligence you uncover. The most successful companies are driving these best practices throughout their organizations. They've earned buy-in and are having constructive conversations about what their markets really look like.

- Set aside your commonly held assumptions about the markets you serve. More than likely, the markets have changed dramatically in the past five years. The data you collect may contradict, or at the very least, challenge what you and your sales team thought you knew.

- And finally, mine the gap. Build systems that allow your sales team to focus their efforts on accounts and segments with the highest potential return. That requires the right incentives, the right training and the right market data. Using market analytics, you can direct your sales team to where the treasure is, and build a team that is smarter and more strategic than your competitors.

About the Author

Thomas P. Gale is president of Gale Media (www.mdm.com), a market-leading information services and publishing company. Its two business units – Modern Distribution Management and MDM Analytics – provide competitive intelligence products and services to professionals in industrial product and wholesale distribution markets. MDM Analytics (formerly Industrial Market Information) provides proprietary market research and analytic services to profile market share and account potential for industrial products. Since 1967, MDM has been the definitive resource for distribution management best practices, competitive intelligence and market trends through its twice-monthly newsletter, market intelligence reports, books and conferences.

Chapter 4

Market Access Analytics:
Use Data to Deploy Sales & Marketing Effectively

Steve Deist, Indian River Consulting Group

Devoting resources to analytics can be a difficult decision because it might mean taking money away from your company's traditional sales force. This chapter will help you navigate that decision and put it into action by underscoring the impact that data can have on a company when it deploys the sales team more effectively and properly aligns resources with market opportunities.

"It's easy to make money in Excel." With these words my colleague Mike Emerson nicely captured the common disconnect between data models and reality. Numeric analysis is a starting point, but it's not an end in itself. A good modelling tool can help us see the impact of raising margins on "loser" customers by a point or getting our fair share of an underdeveloped market, but what it can't do is show us how to actually accomplish those things. That's because numbers don't add up to a plan.

For distributors, the "how to" plan will inevitably involve the sales force, which is usually the biggest single expense category and the most powerful competitive weapon – indeed, the heart of most distributor organizations. This chapter is about translating analytics into action on the front lines of sales and marketing.

Over the past 10 years or so, most distributors have become more data driven and strategic in how they manage their sales resources. There has been a healthy evolution from using only internal, transactional data ("Which customers are down this month?") to working with more external market data and insight ("Where can we realistically grow and where should we harvest?"). **Figure 4-1** summarizes this progression.

Figure 4-1: Sales Evolution

Limited or No Data	Transactional Data	Management Info	Market Insight
• Anecdotes and opinions, little data • Selling is a craft • Priorities set by intuition and interruptions	• Internal sales and financial data • Sales is a process • Priorities set by trends and anomalies	• External market and activity data • Sales is a science • Priorities set by quantified opportunities	• Customer insight • Sales and marketing are sciences • Priorities driven by market goals
Get the order	*Get the customer*	*Target the market*	*Make the market*

As a result of this evolution, world-class distribution organizations are moving toward more specialized selling roles, using hybrid sales reps, specialists, telemarketing, etc. Their sales forces are becoming more management-directed rather than self-directed, and their sales management capabilities are strengthening rapidly. These changes have been very effective, but they require a new level of supporting analytics. For example, to narrow a sales rep's territory so that she is only calling on high-potential customers who value her technical expertise, we have to figure out what the minimum potential should be, how many customers she should have and how they can be identified. This chapter will review some of the proven tools for making these decisions and explain the underlying business logic behind them.

Assessing Market Revenue Opportunity

There's an old military saying: "Most battles are won or lost before the first shot is fired." Combat outcomes are often predetermined by factors like which side has the high ground or where the artillery and cavalry are positioned. We've found a very similar dynamic in the world of distribution. The winners deploy their resources based on a strategy that is aligned to the competitive battlefield. The key word: alignment.

Some customers are truly interested in, but not aware of, a distributor's full set of offerings. Investing in a phone call or promotional email is well aligned with their needs. Some customers may be quite familiar with a distributor as a supplier but may also need extensive technical or business solution support to use the products effectively. Assigning a field sales rep to help them would align with their needs.

Other customers may simply want the product delivered reliably at the best price. Sending a field sales rep to "sell the value" is probably not well aligned with their needs. A competitor who can give them exactly what they want without the cost of what they don't need will ultimately win this battle. Their resources are simply more aligned with the customer's needs.

At Indian River Consulting Group, we refer to the process of aligning resources to market opportunities as "market access." It's not a complex concept, but it has proven to be extraordinarily powerful for our industry. We've found that many companies get stuck because they focus on battlefield tactics ("Are you entering your call reports?") and hand-to-hand combat ("What price do they need?") rather than on the bigger picture issue of how their resources are deployed.

Think about this for a moment, because it's profoundly important. Does it really matter how well trained or highly motivated a sales rep is if the lifetime value of the customer he is visiting is too low to ever cover the cost of his time?

How do we go about aligning our resources? The first step is to understand the macro market opportunities available to us. There's obviously a quantitative aspect to this. As Tom Gale showed in Chapter 3, we can use market data to identify our potential customers and how much they could buy. There's also a qualitative element that is just as important, but harder to measure, which involves understanding the economics and organizational drivers of buying behavior. It's every bit as analytical as market sizing, but it uses tools like executive interviews and focus groups rather than census data and spreadsheets.

There are several different methods for quantitatively sizing markets. The first is customer product gaps, which involves an evaluation of product mix differences for similar customers. **Figure 4-2** illustrates a simplified hypothetical situation.

Figure 4-2: Product Mix

Dollar values in thousands	Employees	Our sales to them, last year					Implied add'l potential				
		Supplies	Services	Widgets	Dongles	Total	Supplies	Services	Widgets	Dongles	Total
Ford Engine Plant	1,000	$10	$10	$10	$10	$40	$0	$0	$0	$0	$0
Chrysler Engine Plant	2,000	$20	$0	$0	$0	$20	$0	$20	$20	$20	$60
GM Engine Plant	5,000	$60	$0	$20	$50	$130	$0	$60	$40	$10	$110
Totals		$90	$10	$30	$60	**$190**	$0	$80	$60	$30	**$170**

Ratio of Ford's Supplies Spend | 100% 100% 100%

In this example, we treat supplies as a "core" product category in which we are most successful across all customers. We also consider Ford to be our best customer, in which our overall share is highest. Ford buys as much of the other categories from us as it does supplies. If we assume that we have a shot at getting this same proportion of other categories from the other two customers, we can derive a rough estimate of our remaining available opportunity for them. Extending this analysis to all customer categories can provide an approximation of the product addressable market (PAM) within our current customer base.

This tool is enticing because it doesn't require any external market data. If we assign customers to groups that should have similar purchase profiles, we can get all the information we need from the transaction data in our order system (typically an enterprise resource planning [ERP] software package). The obvious caveat is that Ford's product mix may not be reflective of other plants, but the information from this tool is often directionally accurate and, at a minimum, can support some interesting sales conversations.

A second tool builds on the first by adding estimates of customer size. We refer to this technique as the internal consumption ratio method because it builds estimates of how much of our product a customer should consume based on headcount, revenue, square footage, number of trucks or some other factor. In the example shown in **Figure 4-3,** we use the number of employees at the engine plants and a best guess of our share at Ford to calculate our PAM for the listed customers.

Figure 4-3: Product Addressable Market (PAM)

Dollar values in thousands	Employees	Our sales to them, last year					Implied add'l potential				
		Supplies	Services	Widgets	Dongles	Total	Supplies	Services	Widgets	Dongles	Total
Ford Engine Plant	1,000	$10	$10	$10	$10	$40	$3	$4	$0	$3	$17
Chrysler Engine Plant	2,000	$20	$0	$0	$0	$20	$5	$33	$29	$27	$94
GM Engine Plant	5,000	$60	$0	$20	$50	$130	$3	$83	$51	$17	$154
Totals		$90	$10	$30	$60	$190	$10	$123	$84	$47	$264
Ratio of Ford's Spend			100%	100%	100%						
Our Share of Ford's Spend		80%	60%	70%	75%						
Implied Consumption/ Head		$0.0125	$0.0167	$0.0143	$0.0133						

Based on our estimates in this example, an engine plant should buy $13 of supplies and $17 of services for each employee. In addition to transactional data, this method requires estimates of our current share at one or more existing customers and information on the relative size of the customer. It's only as accurate as these estimates, but the output is usually sufficiently accurate to draw high-level conclusions on market opportunities.

Most sales reps have at least a few customers for whom they know their true share pretty accurately. If you explain the purpose and of this analysis, sales reps generally don't try to purposely skew the data. After all, if they overestimate a customer's current share, you could question why they spend so much time on it; if they underestimate, you could question their effectiveness. Being accurate is usually the best policy.

A third tool, called location coverage, uses external market data to identify potential new or underserved customers. The market information is a simple business listing that identifies organizations by type (e.g., SIC or NAICS), location and size. For example, it might provide all the automotive plants in the state of Indiana or all the hospitals within a range of ZIP codes. By comparing existing customers against all those listed in the market, we can quickly get a sense of our current market penetration. If we currently sell more than $100,000 to 50 nursing homes and a business list indicates 500 long-term care facilities with more than 100 beds in our geography, we can infer that our current share is around 10 percent.

Although it may seem overly simplistic, this exercise is often eye-opening and can be a useful counterweight to the common refrain from the sales force that "we already know everyone in our market." Strategically, this information can help uncover limitations in coverage and awareness, which may require exploration of additional sales and marketing channels.

The fourth and final tool is external market sizing, which Tom Gale also described in detail in Chapter 3. This method combines consumption ratios with location coverage to estimate the product addressable market. It uses external market data rather than internal transactions to derive consumption ratios, and then applies these ratios to a full listing of applicable businesses in a geography. The math is identical to what is described above for the internal consumption ratio method. A blend of internal and external consumption ratios, along with a location coverage analysis, can provide a very sufficient picture of market share.

Assessing Market Profit Opportunity

Of course, market potential is not just about revenue. Distributors also need to understand their realistic ability to capture the revenue and whether it will generate sufficient profit. While the full process for making strategic decisions about investment, growth and optimization is beyond the scope of this chapter, there are some valuable analytical tools to support it.

Your existing transactional data is an incredibly rich source of information about likely market success and profitability. When combined with some form of activity-based costing (ABC), transactions provide detailed data about the relative profitability of customers, products and business units (branches, regions, etc.).

Indian River Consulting Group has developed a set of tools for visualizing profitability and sales performance information. These enable our clients to identify key patterns and areas warranting deeper investigation. While these tools are proprietary to IRCG, the concepts are something that most readers can apply themselves. The foundational tool is something we call a financial impact tool (FIT), which models the effect that specific changes would have on financial results.

Figure 4-4 Financial Impact Tool (FIT)

	Product Group A	Product Group B	Product Group C	Product Group D	Total
Customer Category 1					
Customer Category 2			Rev: $11M ↑ EBIT: 2.1% →		
Customer Category 3					
Customer Category 4					
Total					

FIT summarizes the current state on three different dimensions: customer groups, product/service categories and business units. For each combination FIT indicates relative revenue size and performance (growth rates), and relative profitability. **Figure 4-4** illustrates a simplified version of this current-state view, showing values for one combination of product, customer and branch.

This visualization has been quite revealing in most cases. Some companies have seen that they were chronically underperforming in the areas of their greatest sales investments, while others learned that what they always considered good business was, in fact, highly unprofitable. At IRCG we often say "data is our friend" because, when properly presented, it helps executives cut through unproductive opinions, stories and cherished beliefs. This type of analysis can truly be a CEO's or CFO's best friend for identifying areas of misalignment and focusing corporate priorities.

Even when the summary doesn't provide any major "aha moments", it provides guidance on where to conduct further analysis on the individual transactions that lie behind each cell in the matrix. For example, if a particular combination is highly unprofitable, a comparison across the product group columns can help us understand if it is largely driven by pricing; a comparison down the customer categories can show the impact of product mix; and a comparison between branches can identify cost-to-serve issues.

Evaluation of customer concentration (the portion of a cell's revenue that comes from a small portion of customers) and churn (the portion of customers that we lose over time) can be exceptionally powerful. If we seem to have issues with value creation or loyalty then it may make sense to focus on sales force effectiveness. If we are struggling with coverage and awareness it may make sense to launch a marketing campaign based on a recency-frequency-monetary (RFM) analysis.

Once we have a clear, organized view of the current state, we can readily model various "what if" scenarios to determine their impact on the company's total revenue and profit. The financial impact tool does this by calculating the impact of combinations of changes in business mix and improvement options.

These tools and models are only as good as the data fed into them. Half-baked or preliminary numbers often tell a very different story than the final set. It's vital that the numbers are reliable, accurate and reasonably precise. We say "reasonably" because it's common to spend too much time attempting to achieve false precision with numbers that are easy to measure while accepting wild inaccuracies with those that are harder to quantify. For example, we've seen companies spend many months fine-tuning their warehouse activity costs but then make the massive assumption that selling activity costs are reflected by commissions paid. For most distributors, selling expense is double or triple that of the warehouse, so if you're going to obsess over precision do it with selling cost! We always recommend some form of time-based cost allocation for the sales force.

No matter how much diligence and cross checking you do, expect that some in your organization will not accept the numbers. They will always be able to find a questionable assumption or oversimplification. Customer profitability analyses are notorious for being rejected by sales reps, who are certain they know which customers are good business. The critics are right: There will be inaccuracies and inconsistencies no matter how hard you work, but the real question is whether it is good enough. As my college statistics professor said: "All models are wrong, but some are useful."

Now that we've explored a range of analytical tools for assessing market opportunity, how do we act on what they tell us? The right approach will be different for every reader, but I can offer some general tips on finding the right answer for your organization. First, determine whether your current markets realistically offer sufficient potential to meet your financial goals in the medium term (say, three to five years out). If they do, then focus your energies on identifying and addressing any misalignments that are preventing you from maximizing sales performance within your current customer base. Business theory says that selling existing products to existing customers is far less risky than trying to learn about new customers or attempting to convince your current customers that you can be good at selling something fundamentally new. Our consulting experience in distribution emphatically supports this theory.

If you conclude that you really must explore new markets, recognize that your success will be hard-fought, so be sure to do thorough market research, a stringent risk assessment and detailed planning. Design controlled experiments or pilots with strict feedback controls and adapt quickly. Try to sell either new products/services to existing customers or your current products/services to new customers. These practices are known as single-adjacency moves because they involve changing a single variable. Trying to sell new stuff to new customers (moving two adjacencies) has a very low probability of success. In distribution, the highest success rate comes from moving core business into new geographies, either through acquisition or green-field start up. Selling new products/services to existing customers is probably second, and attempting to access brand new customer categories or segments is third.

Aligning Resources

Warren Buffett, arguably the most successful businessman of all time, once described himself as "not very talented but born with a God-given ability to allocate capital." Buffett is not really a hands-on manager, and he's never invented anything. Though his folksy charm and wit are endearing, he's hardly a bold or inspiring leader. The secret to his success is his unwavering focus on redeploying Berkshire-Hathaway's assets from less productive uses to more productive ones. He is constantly aligning his resources with market opportunities.

One of the advantages that Buffett has is his detachment from the day-to-day operations of the businesses he owns; he doesn't get too fixated on any particular way of doing things and certainly isn't very sentimental. He's learned that you generally can't fight the tides of markets, even when you've got billions of dollars at your disposal.

Many distributors, especially privately held ones, can learn something from Buffett. It's common for investments in sales and marketing to be based on history or inertia rather than a sober evaluation of the market. We often ask executives: "When was the last time you did a 'clean sheet' design of what your business would look like if you were starting over from scratch?" The answer is often: "I can't remember if we ever really have."

Analytics can help lay the ground work for this type of exercise by painting a clear picture. Let's suppose for example, that we conduct a survey of potential customers (i.e., those that could but are not currently buying from us) and customers we've lost in the past year. We ask them a very simple question: Why are you not buying from us? Possible answers are: they've never heard of us; we've failed them in the past; we don't offer the products or services they need; or we were essentially "outsold" by a competitor.

Figure 4-5: Survey: "Why are you not buying from us?"

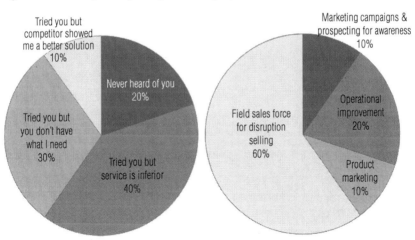

The pie chart on the left side of **Figure 4-5** shows a hypothetical response from our survey. The chart on the right compares these responses with current distributor resources.

The survey responses are fairly evenly spread, with the lowest percentage being customers who were actively lured away by a competitor's sales rep and the highest being customers who found the company's service to be inferior. Compare these responses with how the company actually invests its limited. The majority of its resources are devoted to field sales reps, who attempt "disruptive selling" to convince customers to switch. Operational improvement, which is clearly necessary for improving service levels, receives only a third as much resource. This very simple tool shows that, in this example, the distributor's resources are wildly mismatched to the needs of the market

Of course, this is just an example to show how analytics can help answer a critical strategic question. I'm not trying to imply that the imbalance shown is reflective of any particular distributor, and I would certainly recommend a much more thorough process for assessing customer needs. However, we have observed some consistently large misalignments in resource deployment.

Distributors in many industries are petrified by the threat from Amazon or similar online suppliers, yet they continue to spend less than 1 percent of their revenue on IT. It's probably fair to guess that more than half the readers of this chapter are over-invested in traditional field sales and under-invested in marketing and lower cost sales channels, such as hybrid sales reps.

Cost of Coverage

Analytics can help us determine where and how to apply different sales channels. The fundamental tool for this analysis is a cost of coverage model. Various incarnations of this tool exist, from simple "cost of a sales call" calculations to highly developed models that attempt to quantify the lifetime value of a customer with great precision. For distributors we've found that a good way to begin the evaluation is by looking at sales territories (i.e., groups of customers assigned to an individual sales rep). **Figure 4-6** shows an example of this evaluation.

Figure 4-6: Cost of Coverage Model

Sales Activity	% of Time	Time per Account	Accounts Covered at 2000 Hr/Year	Cost per Try	Close Rate	Cost per Win
Prospects Researching and qualifying to get a foot in the door	5%	4 hours annually	100 hr ÷ 4 hr each = 25	$5K ÷ 25 = $200	5%	$4,000
Closing new business through initial order	5%	10 hours per month for 2 months	100 hr ÷ 20 hr each = 5	$5K ÷ 5 = $1,000	20%	$5,000
Targets Proactively expanding sales (our agenda)	10%	8 hours per month for 6 months	200 hr ÷ 50 hr each = 4	$10K ÷ 4 = $2,500	50%	$5,000
All Relationship, winning sales opportunities (their agenda)	30%	5 hours per month all year	600 hr ÷ 60 hr each = 10	$30K ÷ 10 = $3,000	NA	$3,000
Other (non sales)	50%					
Total	100%	2,000 hours per year		$100,000		

The first column is a breakdown of the key activities of the sales rep. In this example, she is expected to research and qualify prospective customers, get these customers to start doing business with us (i.e., get the first order), proactively target high-potential customers within her territory and maintain relationships with all accounts. In the second column, we enter the portion of her time which we'd ideally like her to devote to each major activity. These add up to 100 percent of the 2,000 hours available each year. The third column shows the rep's estimate of the time typically required per account for each activity. (Don't use commission as a proxy for customer sales cost; you will miss critical insight such as time spent on prospecting and non-customer facing activity.)

The next two columns are simple math-based calculations on time allocation and the rep's total burdened cost of $100,000 per year.

The fourth column essentially defines the number of accounts of each category that the rep can manage. In this example, her territory should consist of 14 accounts plus five active prospects at any given time. The implied territory size for field sales reps is often an order of magnitude smaller than the current state. There is a clear misalignment between what we'd like the rep to be doing (proactively hunting and growing high-potential accounts) and how she is currently deployed (probably spending too much time on big annuity accounts regardless of growth potential and rarely even calling on a high portion of her customers). This misalignment is often driven by commission-based sales compensation plans in which the only way to increase a rep's pay is by adding accounts to her territory. Addressing major resource allocation issues like this are likely to be far more powerful than hiring a motivational sales trainer or implementing voice-to-text call reporting.

The sixth column shows an estimated the win rate for each stage. In this example 5 percent of prospects end up being qualified, 20 percent of qualified prospects give an opening order and 50 percent of target accounts are successfully grown.

Based on these values, it costs the company about $4,800 per year to acquire and hold a prospect for five years:

$4,000	For preliminary research ($200 at 5% success rate)
+$5,000	For closing initial order ($1,000 at 20% success rate)
=$9,000	Total one time acquisition cost
~$1,800	Per year amortized over 5 years
+$3,000	Ongoing relationship and support
=$4,800	Total per year

Based on data from the National Association of Wholesaler-Distributors[1], the average distributor spends about 25 percent of gross margin on sales salaries and commission. So, a prospect must offer the potential for at least $4,800 ÷ 25% = $19,200 per year in gross margin dollars to justify the effort.

These tools and calculations provide a basis for evaluating territory sizes and setting customer assignment criteria. A combination of top-down analysis (How many customers within our geography can justify a sales rep?) and bottom-up analysis (How many accounts can a rep handle?)

---

1 2012 Employee Compensation Report, published by the NAW Institute for Distribution Excellence

Chapter 4 - Use Data to Deploy Sales & Marketing Effectively

can provide a solid, factual basis for the extremely important task of defining new sales roles. These analytical techniques have driven many high-performing distributors to introduce more specialized sales roles. Instead of generic field sales reps, you may find that a combination of inside, hybrid and strategic sales reps can provide both better coverage and more effective target account growth.

Implications for Action

The sales force is the heart of most distributor organizations, so even thinking about re-engineering it can be intimidating. Many executives tell themselves: "We are doing just fine, thanks." and choose to put their efforts into more tactical, lower-risk areas. Unfortunately, the competition is not waiting. As the cost of these analytical tools continues to drop, even smaller companies are using them to gain market share.

At the very least, you should step back and consider how you would deploy the dollars your company spends on sales and marketing if you were starting from scratch. How many potential customers could buy from your company but don't know about you or your offerings? How many existing customers would continue to buy from you – or maybe even buy more from you – if they never saw another salesperson in person? How sure are you about your biggest opportunities for revenue growth? Do you really know how productive your sales reps are? (Hint: You can't find out by looking at their commissions.) These are all questions that your competitors are beginning to answer and act on.

Though numbers will never replace judgment, they have become an essential management support tool. If you are still making sales and marketing decisions based on history, gut instinct or the whiniest sales rep, you are at grave risk of losing out to a more analytical competitor.

Action Steps: Market Access Analytics

- Answer the following questions to create a baseline for a market access strategy:

    - How many potential customers could buy from your company but don't know about you or your offerings

    - How many existing customers would continue to buy from you – or maybe even buy more from you – if they never saw another salesperson in person?

    - How sure are you about your biggest opportunities for revenue growth?

    - Do you really know how productive your sales reps are? (Hint: You can't find out by looking at their commissions.)

- Use the analytical tools described in this chapter and elsewhere in this book to realign sales and marketing resources more effectively.

About the Author

Steve Deist has been an IRCG Partner for six years. He has more than 20 years of experience working for hundreds of distributor, retail, manufacturer and private equity clients in dozens of lines of trade. He is a highly rated speaker, a permanent University of Industrial Distribution faculty member and a distribution company board director.

Chapter 5

Marketing Analytics:
Customer Profiling for Distributors

Jonathan Bein, Ph.D., Real Results Marketing

Analytics can help you profile your customer base and determine which ones are most profitable for your business. This chapter outlines the methods for finding the sweetest spots in your customer base and for managing the entire lifecycle of the customer relationship.

In my experience, distributors routinely have difficulty answering the following two questions:

1. What are the sweetest spots in our customer base?
2. How should we manage the customer lifecycle from first purchase to maturity and beyond?

They may think they have the answers, but often it is based on gut feel or anecdotes. There's no data to back them up. And often, that gut feel is incorrect or, at best, partially incorrect. As a result, distributors may be spending too much effort on some customers while ignoring great opportunities.

The Sweet Spot Problem

When we ask successful distribution executives about the sweet spots in their market, they readily provide a confident answer. But a detailed, analytic look at their customer base shows that some market segments and customers are overrated, some underrated and others are ignored or undetected altogether.

While these executives sincerely believe their answers, there are several reasons why the answers are at odds with data about the customer base. The first is shifting market conditions, such as a downturn or upturn, that changes where the sweet spots are. Segments that were sweet spots at the beginning of the Great Recession or even this decade may not be sweet spots now because the economy has experienced a number of downturns and upturns in that time.

The second reason is that many executives have exposure to only a limited portion of their customer base, often the largest customers. This results in a sampling bias in which they mistake the set of customers they have visited as being representative of the rest of the market.

Finally, many executives know generally which market segments are attractive, but they are unfamiliar with the micro-segments, making it difficult to take meaningful action based on an imprecise classification of customers. One cannot tell who the players are without a scorecard. "Statisticians are not very good informal statisticians," says Daniel Kahneman, the Nobel Prize winner in economics. This is especially true for executives who may have limited statistics background.

Customer Lifecycle Management Problem

One of the biggest challenges for any sales and marketing organization is when to reach out to a customer with an offer or promotion. The objective is to reach out during a natural buying cycle. But reaching out too frequently loses its impact or even turns the customer off, while not reaching out enough could mean losing sales opportunities.

A simple behavioral segmentation technique called recency-frequency-monetary (RFM) value is key to managing the customer lifecycle. It optimizes the timing of offers and promotions without requiring big data to be effective. The main idea of RFM analysis is to classify customers by how recently they have purchased and by how many times they have purchased in a given time period, typically months or years.

Here are the key principles of RFM:

- **"When you're hot, you're hot."** Customers who buy a lot and have bought recently will continue to do so, probably without special offers or promotions.
- **"When you're not, you're not."** Customers who have not bought a lot or who have not bought recently need offers or promotions to get back into a good purchasing pattern.

Effective segmentation and customer profiling allows for targeted messaging to key segments in a language that makes sense to companies in that segment (different industries often use different terminology). Good segmentation also allows for prioritization of customers by sales potential and ease of penetration.

In this chapter, we look at how customer firmographic information – the specific characteristics of a company – and behavioral data can be used to market and sell more effectively to your existing customers.

Sweet Spot Analysis

Our method for finding the sweet spot in a customer base is very simple:

1. Obtain firmographic data on your customers.
2. Gather transaction data on your customers, including annual revenue, gross margin, net profit and orders for each of your customers over a three- to five- year period.
3. Combine the firmographic data with the transaction data to analyze by individual firmographic variables or by pairs of firmographic variables such as line of business and number of employees.

A key premise in this approach is to build on success you are already having in the market. To do that, you must be able to accurately identify where that success really is. Relying on an analyst report that predicts general trends in the market may be true for the industry, but may not apply specifically to your company for one reason or another. Hence, looking at your own information is critical.

Firmographic Variables

Firmographic variables are the specific characteristics of each company, including line of business, annual revenue, number of employees, location and year of founding. Other relevant variables include geography, sales territory, credit rating and the type of account (e.g., regular, cash, COD).

Line of business information usually comes from one of three sources:

1. Common industry classification such as SIC or NAICS.
2. Custom-developed classification or segmentation from your own company.
3. Third-party classification as found in sources, such as Hoovers.

The most reliable approach for analysis exists when a company has developed a good internal classification scheme and applies it consistently to its customer base. In the absence of a good internal classification

Figure 5-1: Revenue and Growth by Line of Business

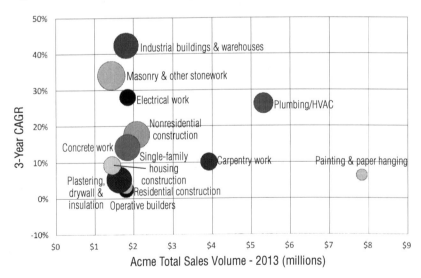

scheme, the common industry approaches or third-party classification schemes work well.

The example in **Figure 5-1** shows revenue volume (horizontal axis) and compounded annual growth (vertical axis) for Acme, a fictitious name for a real company that sells building materials. Before analyzing the data, they believed their best segments were painting and paper hanging, plumbing and HVAC, and carpentry work. The analysis showed that plumbing and HVAC and carpentry work have much higher annual growth rates than painting and paper hanging.

Figure 5-2: Net Profit % and Gross Margin % by Line of Business

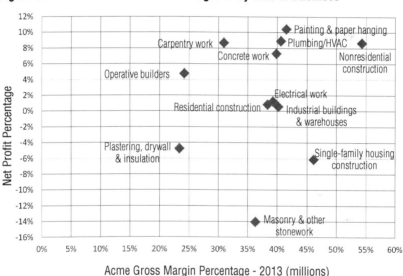

Acme Gross Margin Percentage - 2013 (millions)

Further analysis using gross margin percentage and net profit percentage (see **Figure 5-2**) shows that other segments have attractive profitability, even if they have smaller sales volume. This analysis shows that nonresidential construction is high net profit and high gross margin. From the previous figure, we can see that even though nonresidential construction is a small segment, it is growing at 17 percent compounded per year.

From **Figure 5-2**, we also see that there is very little correlation between gross margin and net profit. Six of the segments in that figure have about 40 percent gross margin, yet the net profit varies for those same segments between 2 percent and 10 percent. Since there is generally very little correlation between net profit and gross profit, it is preferable to use net profit instead of gross profit or revenue in these types of analyses.

When determining the size of a company, we typically look at annual revenue and the number of employees. The reason we look at both variables has to do with the reliability of data either directly from the customer or from third-party sources such as D&B, InfoUsa or Axciom. Most companies are more likely to report their number of employees than their annual revenue.

If you have access to industry-specific measures of size about your customers and prospects, such as number of trucks, technicians or manufacturing employees, that is often the best way to go. It is a more direct way to understand potential opportunity in an account.

Analysis of the size data in **Figures 5-3** and **5-4** shows that Acme has a split between very small companies with less than $1 million revenue

Figure 5-3: Sweet Spots by Customer Revenue

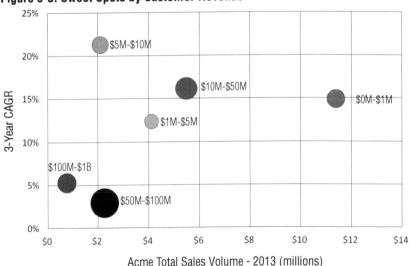

Figure 5-4: Sweet Spots by Number of Employees

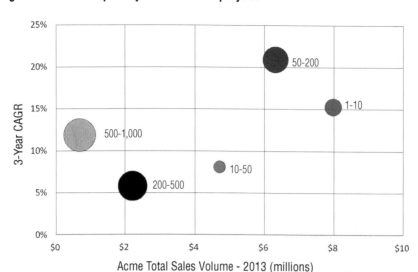

and 10 employees and mid-sized companies with $10 million to $50 million revenue and 50 to 200 employees. At the same time, clients with $5 million to $10 million annual revenue are growing the fastest. However, as the graphs show, Acme has had little success with large corporations.

Year of founding may not seem to be an obvious indicator to everyone, but our work has shown it to be a powerful segmentation variable in several cases. There is not a clear-cut trend for how it correlates to each company; for example, older companies are not always better prospects. In the example in **Figure 5-5**, the highest volume segment for the distributor is companies started in the 1980s.

For distributors who sell to OEMs, we have seen a trend that newer, but not the newest, customers are the best prospects. With another distributor who sells to high-tech companies, its best prospects were founded between 2001 and 2005, yet its worst prospects were founded between 2006 and 2010.

For this distributor, there is a balance in finding OEMs that are new enough to need the distributor's high-tech components but old enough to be successfully selling in-market. For another distributor of green products, its best segments are companies that are environmentally conscious, including new millennium companies, as well as churches and schools that were formed before 1950.

Figure 5-5: Sweet Spots by Year of Founding

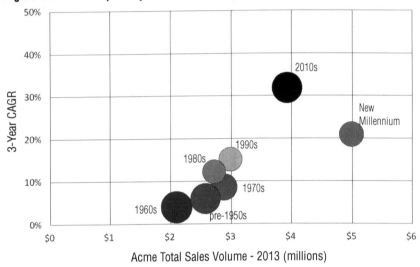

Figure 5-5 shows Acme's customer segments by year of founding. The trend for Acme is clear: Segments with newer companies are higher growth and higher volume than other segments. However, deeper analysis shows that many of the newer companies are smaller, so Acme must align the opportunity in these accounts carefully with cost to serve. It may entail driving those new small accounts to purchase through lower cost channels, such as e-commerce or inside sales, rather than being served by field sales.

Two-Variable Analysis

The examples that we have shown so far are all focused on a single firmographic variable, but it is often useful to work with two variables – for example, line of business and customer revenue. The precision of two-variable analysis is more actionable whether the goal is expanding wallet share or acquiring new customers. Three-variable analysis tends to be too complex and the segments too small to be meaningful.

The best way to get quick sales hits is to know where the existing sweet spots are and to replicate that success. The examples that we included do not require a degree in statistics to understand. Insights leap off the page to even the casual observer.

Besides showing segments where additional sales volume can be easily captured, this method of segmentation can also highlight problem areas. One of our clients who sells HVAC equipment believed that their best segments were HVAC contractors and electrical contractors. While both segments were high volume, the electrical contractor segment actually showed negative growth over a multi-year period.

Upon learning this, the distributor was able to determine whether there was a problem with their offering or service or if it was just the economy. Even more important, we uncovered a segment that, although not as large as HVAC contractors or electrical contractors, was growing at 40 percent per year. The client made significant market gains in that segment with targeted list purchases and marketing campaigns.

Customer Lifecycle Management

When used skillfully in customer lifecycle management, recency-frequency-monetary analysis can drive retention, re-acquisition, and wallet-share programs, as well as optimize promotional spend.

Figure 5-6 contains a point-in-time RFM summary analysis of 21,433 customers from a distributor over a 24-month period. Cells in the upper right portion of the summary represent higher volume customers who have purchased recently. Cells in the lower left of the summary represent low-volume customers who have not purchased recently. In between are various mixtures of sales volume and recency of purchase.

Figure 5-6: Recency Frequency Summary

Customer Count	Months since last order							
Frequency of purchases	13 or more	7 to 12	4 to 6	3	2	1	Totals	%
200 or more	1	1	5	3	12	339	361	1.7%
50 to 199	11	28	29	37	128	980	1,213	5.7%
10 to 49	181	394	677	504	765	1,811	4,332	20.2%
2 to 9	2,390	2,278	1,773	876	951	1,312	9,580	44.7%
1	2,912	1,167	647	341	413	467	5,947	27.7%
Total	5,495	3,868	3,131	1,761	2,269	4,909	21,433	
%	25.6%	18.0%	14.6%	8.2%	10.6%	22.9%		

There are 2,912 customers whose most recent purchase was one year or more and who have only made one purchase in the last 24 months.

There are 339 customers whose most recent purchase is within the last month and who have made at least 200 purchases in the last 24 months.

This RFM summary reveals key things about this company:

- Its most frequent buyers are also among the most recent buyers. In the top row, more than 90 percent of the customers who have purchased 200 times or more have also purchased within the last month.
- Its least frequent buyers – the "one-and-done" customers – represent more than 25 percent of its accounts. Across numerous analyses we have seen that a third to half of one-and-done customers are in a sweet spot segment. That is opportunity walking out the door.
- The accounts that have purchased two to nine times and 10 to 49 times represent the largest segment for this company. Most of these accounts are house accounts that receive very little attention. More than half of these accounts have not purchased in the last three months.

Companies who used recency-frequency-monetary analysis will run the analysis weekly or monthly, often comparing against the previous month to see how sales are trending. If the customer base is increasing in recency and frequency, that is strong evidence the marketing and sales process is going well. In contrast, if overall customers are decreasing in recency, there are likely problems to be addressed.

Figure 5-7: Recency Frequency Monetary Value Summary

Total Spend Trailing 24 Months	Months since last order							
Frequency of purchases	13 or more	7 to 12	4 to 6	3	2	1	Totals	%
200 or more	$ 1,556	$ 87	$ 4,185	$ 924	$ 1,692	$ 219,387	$ 227,832	51.8%
50 to 199	$ 689	$ 5,156	$ 1,991	$ 3,305	$ 7,572	$ 84,151	$ 102,854	23.4%
10 to 49	$ 3,194	$ 5,719	$ 7,885	$ 7,681	$ 12,281	$ 36,169	$ 72,930	16.6%
2 to 9	$ 5,197	$ 6,951	$ 5,523	$ 2,697	$ 3,394	$ 7,743	$ 31,504	7.2%
1	$ 2,156	$ 1,079	$ 560	$ 243	$ 226	$ 537	$ 4,770	1.1%
Total	$ 12,762	$ 18,982	$ 20,144	$ 14,851	$ 25,165	$ 347,987	$ 439,891	
%	2.9%	4.3%	4.6%	3.4%	5.7%	79.1%		

For each cell in the grid in **Figure 5-6**, the corresponding cell in **Figure 5-7** contains the value of the customers in the time period of the analysis. For example, the 339 customers in the upper right cell in **Figure 5-6** have made $227 million of orders during the time period of the analysis. For this distributor and many others, most revenue comes from high-volume customers. The "one-and-done" customers in the first row total only $4.8 million of revenue.

Figure 5-8: Recency Frequency Monetary Incremental Opportunity

Total Incremental Opportunity (000s)	Months since last order							
Frequency of purchase	13 or more	7 to 12	4 to 6	3	2	1	Totals	%
200 or more	$ -	$ 8	$ 70	$ 4	$ 670	$ 9,230	$ 9,982	15.1%
50 to 199	$ 54	$ 77	$ 77	$ 297	$ 493	$ 5,088	$ 6,087	9.2%
10 to 49	$ 687	$ 1,128	$ 1,800	$ 1,301	$ 2,048	$ 4,403	$ 11,368	17.2%
2 to 9	$ 6,939	$ 5,883	$ 4,435	$ 2,171	$ 2,182	$ 2,598	$ 24,199	36.6%
1	$ 7,697	$ 2,762	$ 1,431	$ 735	$ 855	$ 936	$ 14,416	21.8%
Total	$ 15,378	$ 9,858	$ 7,803	$ 4,508	$ 6,249	$ 22,255	$ 66,051	
%	23.3%	14.9%	11.8%	6.8%	9.5%	33.7%		

Real Results Marketing has developed an approach to estimate the incremental opportunity in an account. This can also be used with RFM as shown in **Figure 5-8**. The total estimated incremental opportunity in these accounts is $66 million. By using this information, the company can develop sales and marketing programs to capture the incremental potential in these accounts. By knowing the potential, it also can determine what sales and marketing resources should be applied relative to the opportunity. The distributor might decide to use field sales for only the large accounts, inside sales for the mid-size accounts and e-commerce for the smallest accounts.

Customer Lifecycle Management with RFM

Recency-frequency-monetary analysis provides a straightforward approach for customer lifecycle management. As shown in **Figure 5-9**, each cell has a lifecycle objective. For the most current, high-volume customers, the objective is to serve and maintain the account.

Figure 5-9: Lifecycle Management with RFM

Customer Count	Months since last order					
Frequency of purchase	13 or more	7 to 12	4 to 6	3	2	1
200 or more	Re-acquire	Re-acquire	Re-acquire	Retain	Retain	Serve
50 to 199	Re-acquire	Re-acquire	Retain	Retain	Retain	Serve
10 to 49	Re-acquire	Retain	Retain	Grow	Grow	Grow
2 to 9	Ignore	Retain	Grow	Grow	Grow	Grow
1	Ignore	Ignore	Onboard	Onboard	Onboard	Onboard

The RFM analysis helps detect when a customer is at risk of defection. For example, a high-volume customer who has not purchased in one month or more is at risk of defecting because it normally orders several times per month. The lifecycle objective here is to actively retain the customer through a variety of methods, including offers, additional service, etc. For lower volume customers, it may be several months before retention becomes relevant. At a certain point, the customer has defected and traditional retention methods are no longer applicable, requiring re-acquisition or re-activation.

For some distributors, retention is the main issue. For others, the challenge is to grow small customers into mature customers. We have seen a number of distributors where 30 percent to 40 percent of their customers buy only once or a few times. Some small-volume customers have little potential to become mature customers, but we usually find that within the low-volume customers, there are many who fall into the distributor's sweet spots. Those customers have good potential to grow.

While one-time buyers are technically customers, until they have established a multiple repeat-purchase pattern, they are really a combination of customer and prospect. At this stage of the lifecycle, the customer needs to be brought fully on board. Converting these customers requires a coordinated campaign between sales and marketing to move the customer into the growth stage of the lifecycle. Once customers are there, the objective is to increase orders and order size steadily until the customer is mature and can be handled by field sales or more senior inside sales reps.

Multichannel, Multi-Vehicle RFM

Recency-frequency-monetary analysis has been used as a direct marketing technique for nearly 50 years. At its inception, when postage was four cents, it was used to determine which customers should receive an offer. The determination is made by testing the marketing response rate of the various cells. For example, if we know that the grow cells have a 3 percent to 4 percent response rate, we will include them in marketing campaigns where the breakeven is at 3 percent or lower. If a campaign has a 5 percent breakeven, those cells will not be included. RFM predicts by cell in the grid the customers that are most likely to respond to an offer.

Today, RFM applies not only to print marketing vehicles but also outbound telemarketing, email marketing, Web marketing and even field sales. The breakeven calculation for a campaign now includes the cost for each marketing vehicle in the campaign. Compared to times when print was the only vehicle, the economics of email marketing significantly expands the set of customers who can cost-effectively be touched. Once the contact has been acquired, transmission at less than one cent per contact is extremely affordable.

Even with all of the analytic models available today, RFM remains one of the most powerful methods for predicting campaign response. In contrast to many analytics tools, it does not require significant hardware to run. RFM is easily understood by marketing and sales organizations, and once people get used to the method they become hooked on it. Lifecycle objectives derived from the RFM analysis can be easily integrated into a CRM system so sales reps can take the appropriate actions.

Action Steps: Sales Analytics

- Conduct a sweet spot analysis. This chapter outlines a simple method that is the foundation for better understanding the behavior and trending of your customers.

- Perform a recency-frequency-monetary (RFM) analysis on your transaction data, as outlined here, to create a customer lifecycle management segmentation and strategy.

- Share and discuss the sweet spot and RFM analysis so the management team going forward can base decisions on data, not gut feel about customers and segments.

- Create clear lifecycle objectives for the marketing and sales teams to align activity, including integration into a CRM system to direct appropriate sales rep behavior.

About the Author

Jonathan Bein, Ph.D., is managing partner at Real Results Marketing. Contact him at jonathan@realresultsmarketing.com or visit www.realresultsmarketing.com.

Chapter 6

Sales Analytics:
Focus on the Front End

Brian Gardner, SalesProcess360

Most companies devote time and resources to the back end, the quote and order phases, as opposed to the front end, the lead and opportunity phases. Determining how well your company performs in each phase can identify sales strengths and weaknesses. This, in turn, leads to opportunities for improving sales and maximizing profit.

In the past 30 years of being in the industrial sales world, I have found that most companies manage their businesses from what I call the "back end" of the sales cycle. But shifting the focus to the front end of the sales cycle can have significant value and reward.

At the beginning of my industrial sales career, I, too, was guilty of managing from the back end.

I started in the industrial sales market within a family process control and instrumentation business in the 80s. I had worked through all facets of the business, from sweeping floors, stocking shelves and inside sales to my first outside sales position of calling on C&D accounts (cats and dogs).

When I started in sales, my training was: "Here are your accounts, here is what we sell, and good luck." There was no process to follow or road map to give direction on where to spend my time. The only thing I had was a stack of green-bar sales reports on what had been sold to these

C&D accounts before.

A seasoned sales person at the company who I looked up to took me under his wing and told me: "You have to be in front of the customer, you always have to be looking for opportunities, and you have to do what you say you are going to do and follow up." It sounded pretty simple.

What I found out very quickly was that in sales you can work really hard, but if you don't work smart, you might be spinning your wheels with no new sales to show for it at the end of the day. While calling on those C&D accounts, I figured out that just making sales calls would not get me the top sales person of the year award. I started to figure out that sales was about a process, and I had to figure it out sooner rather than later if sales was going to be my career path.

That summer of calling on those C&D accounts in my first outside sales territory was the building block for my sales success.

It all sounds so simple, but it is often hard for companies to focus on. Why? I believe the answer lies in the past. A lot of companies cling to the ides that "This is the way we have always done it." Another big reason is culture. Companies and individuals hate change, and this change can be difficult as it requires a change in the way the sales team typically works.

First, let's define front end and back end. Think of the sales cycle as a circle, that is a 360-degree process. The back end is the order stage of the sales cycle. The front end is the lead and opportunity stage of the sales cycle.

Each of these is 180 degrees of the 360-degree sales cycle, as shown in the **Figure 6-1**. The analysis in this chapter will follow this 360-degree sales cycle, but in reverse – that is by beginning with the order stage and ending at the beginning of the cycle.

Figure 6-1: Sales Cycle

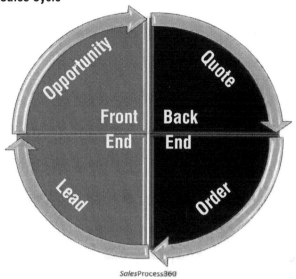

SalesProcess360

Order Stage

Starting with the order stage and working backwards, let's break these four stages down. The following questions will allow you to analyze how your company is doing at each stage and will typically back up my belief that most companies lack focus on the front end of the sales cycle.

Grade your company on the following actions on a five-point scale, with 5 being excellent and 1 being poor.

Order Stage: _____ (Total Average Score)
Order write up standards =
Order retrieval system =
Payment follow-up process =
Reporting (30-60-90) =

1. Order write up standards: Does your company have standards for how orders are written up? Most companies I work with can put 5s on this specific area of the order stage. If you don't have a standardized process for orders, you will probably be out of business soon.

2. Order retrieval system: Does your company have an order retrieval system? Can you put your hands quickly and easily on orders and statuses of orders? I typically find 4s and 5s for this specific area as well.

3. Payment follow-up process: Do you have a process for all your overdue payments for orders? Most companies have a system and process in place for this.

4. Reporting at the order stage: Can you easily get the back-end reports you need? How many orders or payments are 30/60/90 days old? Most companies are usually able to rank this category with 4s or 5s, as well.

Most companies average between 4 and 5 on all of the categories in the order stage. This is how you stay in business, get orders, process orders, get payments and pay your team. It does require some of your focus, but there are other areas that need your focus, as well.

Quote Stage

The next stage on our journey around the 360-degree sales cycle is the quote stage. Again, grade your company on a five-point scale for the following actions, with 5 being excellent and 1 being poor.

Quote Stage: _____ (Total Average Score)
Quote generation standards and procedures =
Quote retrieval system =
Quote follow up process =
Reporting (open, won, lost, overdue) =

1. Quote generation standards and procedures: Do you have standards for what a quote looks like, how to quote and where to document the quote? When Company A gets a quote from your company, does it look the same as the quote Company B received from another person in your company? If your answer is no, then you probably had a low number on your grading on this. In our family sales company, this was the case when I started. Someone at Shell could call wanting a quote for pressure gauges and one of the inside sales team members would generate the quote using his or her own format; the next day another inside sales person would quote the customer in a different format. And that's not even looking at if it was the same price and discount given for the same product.

2. Quote retrieval system: Do you have a process and procedure to organize and store all the quotes being generated in your company? Can you quickly get to all open quotes for a company? Do you know how many quotes were done this week, last month and last year?

3. Quote follow-up process: Do you have a proactive quote follow-up process? Does your team (outside and inside sales) know who is responsible for following up on quotes?

4. Reporting: How quickly can you get a report on your current open quotes? How accurate would that report be? Do you know your quote hit rate (won/lost)?

Most companies average about 3 on the quote stage of the sales cycle. Some do a little better than others on the generation and standards, but most I have worked with fall short on the follow-up process. This is something that is hard for me to understand because if a prospect has reached out for a quote and you have done the work to put the quote together, following up should be an easy next step.

Another potential challenge is companies producing quotes like crazy. I call them "quoting machines." But are they "order-getting machines?" This might go against the grain of sales, but I have coached and consulted companies and seen improved results – higher hit rates, less wasted time and increased sales – by putting every request for quote through a process to determine if that RFQ is worth quoting.

After all, quoting equals time and money.

Here are some things to consider when asked to quote:

- Have we done business with this company before? (If the answer is no, you might want to reconsider or have strong answers for each of the following items.)
- Has this company purchased this product/service before?
- Have we been working with the technical and user buyer on this RFQ?
- Is the product spec'd in or is my competitor spec'd in?
- Are they using me as a third bid? What is our track record over the past 6-12 months of quoting this customer? For example, have we have quoted them 10 times and received no orders?

I challenge you to really look into your quote process and quote pipeline. Start looking at the trends. Create a simple scorecard. Here are some things to keep your eye on:

- Quote input trend by: company, sales person, key products/services, territory, division
- Quotes overdue
- Quote forecast
- Won/lost

The example can serve as a scorecard for each company, salesperson, key products/services, territory and/or division.

Figure 6-2: Scorecard for Quote Stage

Quotes	Load Goals		Month 1	Month 2	Month 3	Month 4	Month 5	Month 6
		Month #						
		Month Total $						
		Total Open #						
		Overdue #						
		Overdue $						
		Forecast						

When you have compiled three months of data into the scorecard, it will become very obvious what is going on or not going on within the sales team and where you need to focus. For the purpose of this scorecard shown in **Figure 6-2**, use the load goal column to create goals. If the monthly number is greater than the goal, put that number in green; if the monthly number is less the goal, put it in red. To avoid making your scorecard look like Christmas, select a range – for example, 20 percent – and if the result falls within that range, put it in black.

Opportunity Stage

The next stage we want to look at is the opportunity stage. Grade your company on a five-point scale for the following actions, with 5 being excellent and 1 being poor.

Opportunity Stage: _____ (Total Average Score)
Opportunity Management system =
Standards for what is an opportunity =
Proactive Follow up process and procedures =
Reporting =

1. Opportunity management system: Do you have a process and system to manage your opportunities? Are you tracking the key items on those opportunities (expected close, next strategic action, competition, etc.)?

2. Standards for what is an opportunity: Does your sales team know what the criteria are for an opportunity? Do you know if the opportunities you are chasing are good opportunities? Remember not all opportunities are good opportunities.

3. Proactive follow up: Do you have a process and system to track the follow-up on your opportunities? Are you tracking the reasons you won/lost opportunities?

4. Reporting: Do you have an accurate opportunity pipeline report? Do you know your percent conversion from opportunity to quote? Can you quickly and easily get a 60/90/120-day forecast? With what level of confidence?

The opportunity stage is probably the most important for growing your business, but I typically find it is the least managed. On average, companies will grade themselves around a 2 at this stage. When you can truly say as management of the company that you are going to defy existing culture and the sales team's reluctance to change and really focus on this stage of the sales cycle, you will find the pot of gold at the end of the sales rainbow. You want to be in the driver's seat with your customers, and managing at the opportunity stage puts you in that position. If you are just managing your business at the quote stage, you are not in control, and, in most cases, your competitor is driving the customer.

Specifications are written at the opportunity stage. The time between opportunities and quoting is the most critical time in the sales cycle. Is your product or service being spec'd in? Or is it your competitors?

Just as we discussed a scorecard at the quote stage, I recommend doing the same thing for opportunities. Here is an example of a simple opportunity scorecard:

Figure 6-3: Scorecard for Opportunities Stage

Opps	Load Goals		Month 1	Month 2	Month 3	Month 4	Month 5	Month 6
		Month #						
		Month Total $						
		Total Open #						
		Overdue #						
		Overdue $						
		Forecast						

Lead Stage

Finally we come to the beginning of the sales cycle: the lead stage.

Again, grade your company on a five-point scale for the following items, with 5 being excellent and 1 being poor.

Lead Stage: _____ (Total Average Score)
Lead generation system =
Lead qualification process =
Lead follow up procedures =
Reporting (Open, Closed, % converted to Opp) =

1. Lead generation system: Do you have a system for generating leads? There are many options for this, including your website, trade shows or email campaigns, just to name a few.

2. Lead qualification process: Once you get a lead, is there a qualification process? I typically find that when the lead comes in, regardless of source, it is simply forwarded to the sales person. There are no qualification processes in place to determine if it is a qualified lead or not. The sales person shouldn't be sitting around waiting for leads to come in as they're already working other qualified opportunities and following up on existing quotes. As a result, often the lead just sits and never goes anywhere. Maybe a couple of weeks later the sales person finally gets around to the new lead and finds out he is late to the party.

The companies that effectively manage leads are ones that have processes in place to qualify leads before they even get to the sales person. They have established the questions they need to find answers for before it moves to the next stage or next person in the company. For example:

- Why is the person inquiring about your products or services?
- How did they find out about your company and products?
- Is there an approved project or funds for your products or services?

3. Lead follow-up procedures: Are there follow-up procedures for qualifying the leads? Is there a system to document the information you obtain? Once the lead has gone through the qualification process and is turned over to the sales team, are there procedures and systems to make sure the sales team is following up on the leads and either closing them or moving them to the opportunity stage?

This is a big part of a successful lead management process. The sales team needs to know that the company is spending time and resources to qualify the lead, rather than just forwarding every lead and expecting the sales team to take it to the next level. Put a check-and-balance system in place. If you are seeing that leads are being qualified based on your process and the sales team is not converting the leads to opportunity stage, you will need to review the process and figure out where the problem or miscommunication lies.

4. Reports: Do you have a system to track and monitor the leads that are coming into your company? Key areas you should be tracking are:

- Source (make sure you are getting marketing ROI)
- Product/service
- Number of leads
- Qualification days
- Percent converted to opportunity

Most companies average around 1 and 2 at the lead stage. Companies often get the leads and forward to the sales team with no system to track and manage. They put the responsibility on the sales team to qualify them, and hope that the sales team moves that lead to the opportunity stage.

Implications for Action

Most companies are managing their businesses from the back end of the sales cycle, but they are missing the value and opportunity that can come from shifting some of that focus to the front end. **Figure 6-4** represents the typical grades I receive from the audiences at the seminars I conduct.

Your results may be different then what I typically see, and if your results are higher on the front end, I applaud you. You and your company are ahead of the curve. But don't stop there. Really analyze this within your company. Get your team to do this exercise and see how they grade the company. Document your workflow from lead to opportunity to quote to order. Then do this exercise again and see if you come up with same score.

Figure 6-4: Diagram of Typical Grades

SalesProcess360

In the beginning of my sales career, I was guilty of focusing on the back end of the sales process, as was our entire industrial sales team. Our scores were at or worse than the average at each of the stages. We didn't have a lead management process, we were not doing opportunity management, there were no real quote generation standards, and our quote follow-up process was nonexistent. We got some nice green bar sales reports out of the IBM system36 accounting software every month that showed what orders were invoiced, but that was about it.

We had to change in order to grow our business. That change started with putting a focus on the front end of the sales cycle by changing our culture. When we started this change we were a $10 million company; a little more than six years later, we were a $30+ million company. To this day, I believe one of the major factors was the focus put on the front end of the sales cycle. The processes, procedures and visibility we put on this were driven by management through the organization.

Not everyone was drinking the Kool-Aid on these changes right from the beginning. The expectations and requirements we demanded from the sales team took some employees out of their comfort zones. They were not used to the documentation and follow-up processes we expected and inspected, but once we starting having success it became a much easier sales pitch to the team and ultimately became the new culture.

Action Steps: Sales Analytics

- Don't look at doing this unless management is ready to lead the charge. This is going to require a change in culture in most companies: "No pain, no gain."

- Start with shoring up your back end first. The easiest place to start is with your quoting process. Put in place a quote follow-up system with your sales team. Start tracking won/lost and why. Make sure the expected close dates are accurate. This will give you a pipeline you can use to manage inquiries. Expect and inspect that your sales team will take responsibility of managing the quote process.

- Once the sales team is doing quote follow up and it has become part of the culture, move to the opportunity stage. Put in place a simple opportunity management system. Get the sales team to start documenting the opportunities they find that are ahead of the quote stage and ones they will need to work on to bring to the quote stage. This can start as a simple spreadsheet with columns representing the key information they need to capture – and frankly should be asking anyway. Here is an example of some key information your salespeople need to obtain and document:

• Date	• Expected Close Date
• Company	• Next Action
• Contact	• Next Action Date
• Product	• Status
• $ Potential	

With just this basic information you can:

- Trend the input of what is being created by your sales team.
- Get an opportunity pipeline report.

- Get accurate forecasting by date range; look at your 30/60/90-day forecast.
- See the focus of the sales team by product/service, making sure they are spending the time on the products they should be focused on.

- Once you have made opportunity management part of the culture within the company, tackle the lead stage. Review all the sources for how you are getting leads. Put those leads into a tracking system or spreadsheet. Put in place a qualification process to have someone qualify the leads via a standard questionnaire before turning over to your sales team. (See the question examples under the lead stage section.) This will give confidence to the sales team that when they get a lead, it is truly qualified. It will also give you more accurate feedback on what sources are producing the best leads so you can make sure you are spending marketing dollars in the best place.

This does not have to be complicated. Keep it simple. Put processes, procedures and visibility at each of the four stages of the sales cycle and make sure those processes and procedures are followed.

The goal is for your company to grade each of the stages with 4s and 5s and create a culture with a focus on the front end of sales.

About the Author
Brian Gardner is taking his passion for process improvement to the speaking and coaching world as the founder and lead evangelist at SalesProcess360. Gardner has spent more than 25 years in sales and sales management in the industrial market. He served as sales manager for a major regional rep/distribution company for 15 years before founding Selltis, LLC – the only industrial focused sales team CRM solution with roots deeply embedded in sales process improvement.

Chapter 7

Pricing Analytics:
Analytics for Distributor Pricing & Cost to Serve

Brent Grover, Evergreen Consulting, LLC

The right pricing strategy is critical for a distributor that wants to remain competitive, but too many companies take the wrong approach to pricing, usually focusing simply on gross margin, volume or whatever the market will bear. This chapter shows the importance of taking away the pricing latitude typically given to sales reps and instead applying analytics to devise the right price.

Does your distribution business have a pricing strategy? If so, it might be based on one of these approaches:

- Pricing somewhat above competition due to superior value proposition (focus on profit)
- Pricing somewhat below competition to leverage lower operating costs (focus on volume or share)
- Pricing at whatever market will bear

Each of these examples requires some knowledge of the market prices for the products you sell. But how do you know what those market prices really are? Applying pricing analytics to your pricing strategy can help make this determination.

Pricing analytics is a systematic series of basic computations of your 12 most recent months of customer transactions on a line-item level – a big set of data, to be sure. It begins with dividing your pricing into its constituent elements, represented by these four data elements:

- Who is this customer? What customer pricing segment is this customer in?
- How much business does this customer do with us?
- What product is the customer buying?
- How sensitive is this customer to the price of this product?

These computations will reveal how much customers of various sizes in different segments pay for individual products and product groups. The tabulation also takes into account non-statistical information such as your opinion of which products' prices are highly visible and your awareness of competition and customer preferences.

The results enable you to eliminate pricing outliers (below-market pricing) and create pricing matrices that truly reflect market pricing. When properly implemented, you will sustain margin gains and build upon them without losing profitable business.

Why Analytics is Critical to Manage Pricing & Profitability

Distributors customarily delegate more pricing responsibility to their sales teams – both outside and inside – than almost any other industry. The irony is that most companies report a strong positive correlation between profit performance and management influence over pricing. In other words, profits are lower when management has loose controls over pricing.

Distributor sales reps traditionally enjoy some features of being in business for themselves, such as the ability to set their own schedules and to choose which customers to work most closely with and which products to promote hardest. The feeling of independence is underscored by a sales compensation plan often based largely or entirely on gross margin dollars.

This latitude given to distributor sales reps often extends to quoting prices. A typical distributor pricing practice is probing what the "traffic will bear" by quoting a price, getting a customer reaction and being prepared to meet the competition, if possible. The initial price offer may be based on an arbitrary discount from a list price, a price book bracket price or a gross margin percentage applied to the product's standard cost – a cost determined by management, not inclusive of rebates, cash discounts or special deals, but including freight.

Figure 7-1: Distributor Pricing Diagram

This practice presents two crucial variables. First, the sales rep is mostly just guessing, based on anecdotal information, what the competitor's price might be. The other variable is the rep's willingness to let a competitor, real or imagined, set the price so long as it is somewhat above the standard cost. For large pieces of business, the competitive situation may cause the sales rep to ask his company's management or a supplier for a special cost to capture the business.

At best, the seller's initial price offer, and the ensuing negotiation with the customer, is based on educated guesses; often it is based entirely on the rep's hunches. Below-market pricing or pricing outliers, happen when the initial offer is less than what the customer is willing to pay. When the customer responds with a competitive offer, the distributor sales rep's counteroffer (meet or beat the competition) remains below what the customer is willing to pay.

"Win-win" negotiations don't work when one person can see the cards and the other person has no cards. Negotiation without information isn't good for profits.

Distributor sales reps need market pricing information, including what similar customers pay, to make a realistic offer and to be ready to make a counteroffer if necessary. The temptation to meet or beat the competition results in the proverbial "race to the bottom" unless the sales rep knows the market price. If it's necessary to come down from the original offer as part of the negotiation, the seller should ask for a concession, such as larger quantity, long-term commitment or additional items on the order, in return. The willingness to come down should also be tested against what other customers like this one (same segment and size) pay for this item or others like it. The distributor's standard cost for the product has little to do with its value to the customer.

Figure 7-2: Distributor Strategic Profit Model

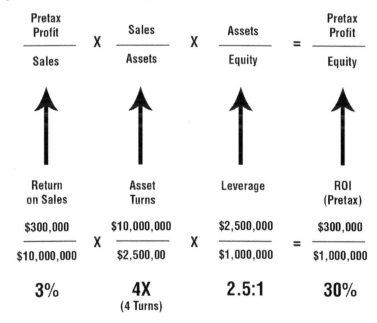

$\dfrac{\text{Pretax Profit}}{\text{Sales}}$	X	$\dfrac{\text{Sales}}{\text{Assets}}$	X	$\dfrac{\text{Assets}}{\text{Equity}}$	=	$\dfrac{\text{Pretax Profit}}{\text{Equity}}$
Return on Sales		Asset Turns		Leverage		ROI (Pretax)
$\dfrac{\$300,000}{\$10,000,000}$	X	$\dfrac{\$10,000,000}{\$2,500,00}$	X	$\dfrac{\$2,500,000}{\$1,000,000}$	=	$\dfrac{\$300,000}{\$1,000,000}$
3%		4X (4 Turns)		2.5:1		30%

A small change in selling price, whether up or down, makes a big difference in the distributor's profits. The distributor strategic profit model illustrates the magnifier effect of asset turnover and leverage.

A modest increase in margin – 1 percent (100 basis points) in the example used in **Figure 7-2** on the previous page – increases the distributor's return on sales by about the same percentage. But this seemingly insignificant bump in margin increases the company's return on investment by 10 percentage points, from 10 percent to 20 percent. The magnifier effect results from the distributor's high asset turnover (sales divided by assets) of four times and the company's leverage (assets divided by equity) of two and a half times. In other words, a small percentage change in margin increases ROI by a factor of 10.

There is no change that management can make – sales increase, expense reduction, faster turns of inventory or receivables – that compares with the ROI opportunity of optimizing margins.

The Competitive Gap

Profit Planning Group has been producing PAR Reports for more than 40 distributor trade associations for almost 40 years. A review of PAR Reports from various distributor lines of trade reveals gigantic profit performance differences between the top-quartile profit performers and median performers. This performance gap has been seen over the years across all trade lines.

Notice that the PAR Report data does not support the idea that distributors with higher margins always make more profits than distributors with lower margins. We often find that distributors with high margins suffer from high operating expenses as the direct result of a small-order problem – the result of a poorly designed business model. A focus on small customers coupled with a high operating cost structure simply is not a good combination.

That being said, optimizing margins and fixing outliers is always a good idea, no matter your business model.

Measuring customer profitability and figuring out the root causes of profits and losses is absolutely necessary when optimizing prices. High-profit customers don't always have high margins. Their excellent results may be a combination of large order size and low cost to serve. Large-loss customers may have high margins, but their losses may be caused by small orders and high cost to serve. We can't jump to conclusions about pricing until we understand the situation with each customer.

Customer profitability can be depicted as a three-legged stool: margins, order size and cost to serve.

Figure 7-3: Three-legged Stool - margin, order size, cost to serve

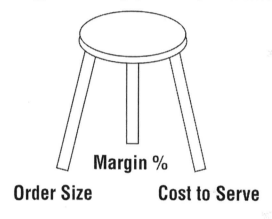

Margin %

Order Size   **Cost to Serve**

A profitable customer is usually a balance of the three factors. For example, if order size is small, higher margins and lower cost to serve compensate for it.

Ranking customers from most profitable to least profitable makes it easy to divide customers into four groups: high profit, low profit, small loss, large loss. If you're using a four-quadrant square, the profitable customers make up the top two quadrants, and the money-losing customers comprise the bottom two. The large-profit and large-loss customers go on the right side, and the small-profit and small-loss customers go on the left, as seen in **Figure 7-4** on the next page.

Figure 7-4: Customer Quadrants

Low Profit	High Profit
Sizable Portion of Profits Large Number of Accounts **Build These Accounts**	Large Portion of Total Profits Small Number of Customers **Protect These Customers**
Sizable Amount of Losses Large Number of Accounts **Work On These Accounts** **Small Loss**	Large Portion of Losses Small Number of Customers **Fix These Customers** **Large Loss**

Analyze the quadrants by breaking them down into their constituent elements: margin percentage, order size and cost to serve. Consider adding some additional elements, such as lines per order. Your analysis will demonstrate the root causes of profit and loss for your customers. This exercise can be repeated for groups of related customers, sometimes referred to as customer families, if looking at the individual accounts isn't meaningful enough.

The exercise demonstrates that some of your high-profit customers have strong order sizes and low cost to serve but not necessarily the highest margins. Fixing their pricing outliers is a good idea, but do so patiently and with care. The large-loss customers may have serious issues with order size and cost to serve, but their margins may not be the root cause of their loss situations. If customers are already paying market prices, the way to turn the losses into profits isn't to implement blanket price increases.

Future State: Better-Informed Management Takes Control

Distributors are under profit pressure as both customers and vendors try to shift more costs to the distributors. Examples of additional work and costs include technical support, credit card processing fees, rebates, equipment repairs and maintenance, product training and warranty service.

The distribution industry hasn't been very successful in unbundling the costs of value-added services from product prices. Customers and suppliers are resistant to accepting fees from distributors for additional services. Efficiencies from newer technologies are providing some opportunities to increase people productivity in distribution, but distributors can't rely solely on increased productivity to pay for additional services for customers and suppliers.

Al Bates, president of Profit Planning Group, says PAR Report data show that the distribution industry's pretax return on assets has been fairly steady over many years, averaging about 7 percent (rising and falling in a range of about 4 percent to 10 percent depending on the economic cycle). If the return on assets is destined to decline in the future, how will distributors attract capital? On the other hand, shouldn't investors in the distribution industry expect return on assets of better than 7 percent?

Competition alone is not preventing distributors from passing additional costs along to customers. Other factors include:

1. Margins in wholesale distribution are depressed in large measure because of delegation of pricing decisions without market pricing information.
2. Order size, a profound indicator of profitability, is not given enough emphasis due to a lack of understanding of its importance.
3. Cost to serve, which varies widely from customer to customer, is not measured and managed.

Try to imagine a future state in which better-informed management takes more control over margins, order size and cost to serve.

The whale curve, introduced in Chapter 2 and again in **Figure 7-5**, plots the distributor's cumulative profit. The vertical axis is cumulative profit or loss dollars, and the horizontal axis is customers, from highest profit on the left to largest loss on the right. The line, depicting a whale, slopes up sharply with the accumulated profits from the high-profit accounts. Then it flattens out as it moves to the right, peaking and then falling off due to money-losing customers. The sharp drop-off at the far right shows the effect of some large-loss accounts. The peak of the curve is the company's earnings potential if all customers were profitable; the far right is actual earnings.

Figure 7-5: Whale Curve Illustration

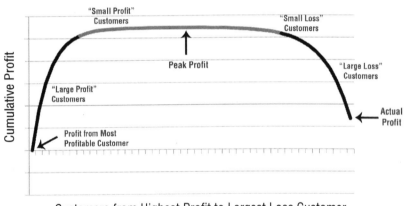

Customers from Highest Profit to Largest Loss Customer

Optimizing margins, in addition to managing order size and cost to serve, attacks the problems at the far right side of the whale curve and brings the actual results much closer to the peak.

Managing Pricing & Customer Profitability

Distributors can achieve better management by using analytics to manage the different pieces.

Let's walk through the process step by step:

Download the most recent line-item level transaction data, preferably a full 12 months to avoid seasonal distortions. Capture all data fields you will want to sort on in your analysis, such as customer name, territory, branch, customer segment, customer size, order type, price, cost, etc.

Separate the transaction data into its components. Use the data fields to sort the line items by customer. Determine the typical margin percentage for each of your many product groups by customer segment and by customer size strata within the segments.

Analyze how sensitive customer segments are to each product group by determining what portion of customer dollars are spent on each group. Examine larger accounts closely to identify which specific products are the most sensitive ones to those accounts. Validate the analysis with management knowledge of the customers, competition and marketplace visibility of pricing.

Identify outliers. Compare the typical margins paid by customers in each segment and size strata with the actual prices paid by individual customers. Identify situations where customers are paying less than comparable customers (same segment and size). Identify patterns and underlying causes of the pricing outliers.

Build market-driven matrices. Use the pricing analysis to create data-driven pricing matrices that reflect actual market pricing by customer segment and size for each product group.

Develop an implementation plan for addressing the pricing outliers for each customer in each sales territory.

Measure, sustain and build margins. Now that the analytics have "come to life," it's necessary to generate exception reports to track implementation of the outlier elimination plan as well as monitoring price quotes versus matrix pricing.

Perform a detailed analysis of the company's profit & loss statement to break each expense line down into the functional areas of the business (sales, sales support, office, handling, etc.). Determine the basic cost to serve for each of the company's order types (warehouse, direct, counter, service).

Apply the basic cost to serve by order type to the trailing 12-month transaction data. Reconcile the company's cost of goods sold per the financial statements with the cost of goods sold used in the transaction processing system.

As the final step in the analysis, **identify major data elements that contribute to cost-to-serve differences** from one customer to another.

Implement corrective action on customer and customer group level. Group the customers into quadrants: large profit, small profit, small loss and large loss. The objectives and tactics for each quadrant will be different. The primary objective for large-profit customers – the small group of accounts that generates much of the company's profits – is to protect the customers at all costs. For small-profit customers – a long list of accounts – the principal goal is to build the accounts. The small-loss customers, also a long list, need a great deal of work (building order size, optimizing margins and reducing cost to serve). Finally, the short list of large-loss accounts generates most of the company's losses. These accounts require a strong effort by management and sales staff to turn the accounts around.

Measure, sustain and improve order size and cost to serve. Profit and loss statements are not only for customers. The analysis includes determining the P&L for sales territories, branches, customer families and customer segments. Examining the data will uncover patterns, root causes and corrective actions.

Don't be intimidated by the list of steps; it's meant to make the process as understandable as possible. And having the right tools in place will make it easier, as well.

Analytics Tools Required

My first experience with measuring distributor customer profitability and pricing analytics was in the 1980s at a seminar hosted by the Chicago-based consulting firm A.T. Kearney. The experts from Kearney demonstrated a project they conducted for an enormous distributor client American Hospital Supply Company.

The enabling technology was large-scale computing power (IBM System 360) available only to the largest companies. The transaction database from American Hospital Supply had to be mapped and exported to custom software for Kearney's system. Typical distributors at that time had neither the computing power nor the programming capability.

Another bottleneck was activity-based costing, a tool designed for manufacturing businesses but not useful to distributors, which was viewed as state-of-the-art for the process.

Now, more than 30 years later, those bottlenecks are gone. Distributors of all sizes have access to the computing power, software and analytics tools to mine their data for market pricing and customer profitability information.

Technology

ERP systems: Exporting 12 months of line-item transaction data takes only a short time to set up and a few minutes to complete. The data export can be repeated as often as needed as a batch process, or in real time if desired.

Microsoft Excel: The capacity, speed and flexibility of Excel is adequate for many of the pricing analytics and customer profitability analysis applications. Most distributors have staff with a good working knowledge of Excel features, such as pivot tables and graphing.

Access, Crystal Reports, SQL: Although they are not essential for most projects, advanced data analysis and reporting tools are readily available and affordable. These three programs are just examples of what's available.

Skill Sets

Management: Most of the distributor leaders we work with appreciate the need for data-driven decision making. More CEOs, CFOs and others use business intelligence tools such as Cognos, MITS and Phocas.

Account executives: The complexity of sales rep technology has increased at a rapid rate. The transition of the sales profession to become more of a "knowledge worker" job, rather than only a product subject matter expert, limits the ability of some sales reps to accept strategic pricing and to evaluate their customers on the net profit level. The technology gap has become more apparent as the median age of distributor sales representatives has risen over the past 10 years.

Pricing coordinator and pricing team: Our experience in implementing strategic pricing and customer profitability analysis with hundreds of distributor management teams and sales forces is that successful behavior change is a team effort. A cross-functional team includes leaders from finance, sales, IT, operations, HR and marketing (if it is a separate function). We also recommend designating an experienced manager as the company's pricing coordinator.

Culture Shift

Business strategy and pricing strategy: A recent McKinsey survey indicated that 97 percent of CEOs placed a high value on strategic thinking by their managers. We see a vital link between a distributor's overall business strategy and its pricing strategy. The pricing strategy and the company's commitment to building customer profitability is expressed through its business processes (How do we determine selling prices?) and its compensation programs (How do we incentive our sales reps?).

Leadership: If leadership is all about getting people to do things they don't want to do, behavior management begins with management doing things it doesn't want to do. As consultants, we work hard to nudge CEOs and other leaders out of their comfort zones. When pricing projects and customer profitability initiatives don't bear fruit as fast as expected, the problem usually starts when people at the top aren't willing to take some measured risks.

Relevance: Culture shifts are a daunting task. Some people, such as sales reps who can't adapt to newer technologies, just can't make it. The challenge isn't limited to sales reps or to baby boomers; they just stand out in the distribution industry because about one-third of the staff is in sales and the industry has seen low turnover in recent years. There is also no doubt that the sales rep job description has changed significantly in the past decade.

Success Stories - Case Studies

Case #1: Packaging and janitorial suppliers distributor

The president of a $200 million regional business persuaded the board to go along with a customer profitability analysis and pricing analytics. The information revealed why some of the company's largest customers were unprofitable. Decisive management action turned those accounts around and delivered a 200-plus basis point increase in gross margins.

Case #2: Steel and metal products distributor

The management team of a more than $100 million multiregional distributor was buried under a myriad of data. Pricing and cost-to-serve analytics helped ensure that each delivery route was profitable by increasing order sizes, reducing cost to serve and increasing margins with new market-driven pricing matrices.

Case #3: Floor covering distributor

Analytics helped a regional company increase margins and order size while reducing cost to serve. The analysis led to revamping of the sales compensation program to focus on operating profit instead of gross margin and volume.

Case #4: Food ingredients distributor

The CEO of $100 million regional business was concerned that pricing analytics wouldn't work in the company's hotly competitive market for commodities. After much reflection he launched a strategic pricing plan. Within three months, 80 percent of quotes were at or above matrix pricing. The company achieved a 300 basis point increase (3 percentage points) on new quotes and 50 percent increase in gross margin dollars on smaller orders.

Case #5: Tire distributor

The general manager of a $50 million specialty tire company convinced the CEO to try a strategic pricing experiment. The managers felt that pricing in the brand-name tire business was too transparent for strategic pricing to work. After a short time the company achieved a 200 basis point margin increase on many of its product lines.

Case #6: Industrial supplies distributor

The owner of a regional company with more than $100 million in annual sales felt locked into the pricing structure of his major supplier and many national contracts. Pricing analytics uncovered opportunities to increase margins by more than 300 basis points for some products. Customer profitability and cost to serve data turned a large loss from absorbing outbound freight costs into an excellent profit center by passing freight costs along to many customers.

Implications for Action

"When it comes to the prices we pay, we study them, we map them, we work on them. But with the prices we charge, we are too sloppy!" complained Jeffrey Immelt, General Electric CEO, in 2006.

Distributors aren't the only businesses struggling with managing pricing. In 2011, Simon-Kucher & Partners studied how 3,900 decision-makers in many industries all over the world set their prices. They determined that pricing power is largely untapped.

Our observation is that pricing is the most lightly managed – or most under-managed – function within even the best-run wholesale distributors. As mentioned earlier, there is a positive correlation between management control of pricing and profitability. And for distributors there is enormous leverage between a small change in gross margin percentage and a large increase in ROI percentage.

Action Steps: Pricing Analytics

Eliminating pricing outliers and building market-driven pricing matrices, coupled with building order size and managing cost to serve, must be one of the first things you do with analytics.

- Use analytics to tighten some of the latitude your sales reps currently have in pricing. Profits are lower when management has loose control over pricing.

- Make sure distributor sales reps have solid market pricing information, including what similar customers pay, so they can make a realistic offer and to be ready to make a counteroffer if necessary. The temptation to meet or beat the competition results in the proverbial "race to the bottom" unless the sales rep knows the market price.

- Don't jump to conclusions about pricing until you understand the situation with each customer. Measuring customer profitability and figuring out the root causes of profits and losses is absolutely necessary when optimizing prices.

- Try to imagine a future state in which better-informed management takes more control over margins, order size and cost to serve. Then follow the step-by-step process outlined in this chapter to better manage pricing and customer profitability.

- Don't underestimate the culture shift required and necessary actions to implement what the analytics show. When pricing projects and customer profitability initiatives don't bear fruit as fast as expected, the problem usually starts when people at the top aren't willing to take some measured risks.

About the Author

Brent R. Grover founded Evergreen Consulting in 2001 as a boutique firm to advise companies in the wholesale distribution channel. He had been CEO and co-owner of National Paper & Packaging Co. Brent is also an Adjunct Professor at Case Weatherhead School of Management. Before his distribution industry career he was with Arthur Andersen & Co. Brent can be reached at brent@evergreen-consulting.com. Visit Evergreen Consulting at www.evergreenconsultingllc.com.

Chapter 8

Inventory Management Analytics: Maximize Productivity & Profitability

Jon Schreibfeder, Effective Inventory Management

Analytics can help your company see where it is meeting or falling short of customer expectations and how it can most effectively manage inventory. Incorporating metrics into your business plan will streamline inventory, maintain the right products on hand at the right time, keep customers happy and – most importantly – maximize productivity and profitability.

The goal of effective inventory management is to meet or exceed customers' expectations of product availability with the amount of each item that will maximize your next profits. Several metrics can help monitor your progress in achieving this goal:

- Customer service level
- Monitoring stockouts
- Inventory turnover
- Turn/Earn (T/E) Index
- Gross margin return on investment (GMROI)
- Three-way ranking
- Percentage of excess inventory

Customer Service Level

The customer service level measures how often you have the items you've committed to stock when your customers want them. If you don't have what your customers want, they must look for it elsewhere.

Your competitors won't have to make sales calls; your customers will seek them out.

The customer service level is calculated with the following formula:

$$\frac{\text{Number of line items for stocked products shipped complete in one shipment by the promise date}}{\text{Total number of line items for stocked products ordered}}$$

In this formula, we measure line items shipped complete. That is when the entire quantity ordered is delivered in one shipment on or before the "promise" date listed on the order. If the customer orders 10, and we ship 10, we get credit toward the customer service level. But if the customer orders 25 and we ship only 24 before the promise date, we get no credit. It is a pass-fail test.

Why no partial credit for shipping 24 out of 25? If the customer wanted 24, he or she would have ordered 24. They want 25. The customer still needs to find that last item somewhere else – probably at your competitor's warehouse down the street. Or they have to wait (and perhaps delay a project) for you to receive a replenishment shipment.

Why no credit if we deliver the quantity in more than one shipment? Your customer has to process multiple stock receipts, and your firm has to process multiple shipments to complete the order. Both parties incur additional costs with multiple shipments.

When calculating your customer service level, we include sales only of stocked items that are filled using warehouse inventory. We don't include:

Special order or non-stock items – Items that you do not keep on hand but are specially ordered to fill a specific customer order.

Direct or "drop" shipments – Material sent directly from a vendor to your customer.

Shipments of these types of items do not reflect how well you stock material to meet your customers' immediate needs. Companies who include special order items and direct shipments when calculating a customer service level tend to overstate how well they serve their customers from warehouse inventory.

Recording Out-of-Stock Situations

The customer service level is a great measurement, but it is dependent on two factors that are sometimes hard to control:

- Salespeople accurately recording the promise date for each line item on a customer order.
- All customer requests for products being accurately recorded.

One of our clients had salespeople who continually defaulted the promise date on every customer order to the current date even though the firm delivered most orders the next day. Because most orders were delivered after the recorded promise date, their computer system considered nearly every line item late, which resulted in a very low customer service level even though deliveries generally met customers' expectations.

At another company, customer requests for products that were completely out of stock were not recorded. If a customer ordered 10 pieces of a product and only one piece was shipped in the initial shipment, the transaction negatively affected the customer service level. But if the item was completely out of stock, no order was entered so there was no effect on the customer service level.

To avoid these problems, some companies measure stockouts as an alternative to the customer service level. A stockout occurs when the available quantity of a product (on-hand quantity minus quantity committed on current orders) falls to or below zero.

When this situation occurs:

- The number of stockouts for the product is incremented by one.
- The date of the stockout is recorded.

When a stock receipt for the product is entered into the computer system and the available quantity rises above zero, the date of the end of the stockout is noted and a "days out of stock" for the current month is incremented by the length of the stockout.

It is imperative that both the number of stockouts and days out of stock are recorded each month for each stocked item because they tend to identify two very different problems:

Number of stockouts: If a popular A-ranked product experiences many stockouts (e.g., more than two in a four-month period), it probably means that its normal reorder quantity is too small. All or most replenishment shipments are used to fill back orders that have accumulated during the lead time. The standard reorder quantity of the product needs to be increased to satisfy customer demand between replenishment shipments.

Days out of stock: This is a situation where the number of stockouts is low but an item has been out of stock for a significant number of days within the past several months (e.g., 14 days within a four-month period). This usually is the result of an inconsistent lead time or other vendor problem.

Some companies consider an item to be out of stock when the available quantity drops below the average or typical order quantity. For example, if customers normally order a dozen of a certain fastener at a time, having only one or two pieces on the shelf may be the equivalent of having none.

Analyzing the Customer Service Level and Stockouts

Best practice is to analyze either customer service level or stockouts each month using several criteria including:

Rank of product – A-ranked products usually make up 80 percent of product requests or 80 percent of the cost of goods sold. These are the products that customers request most often and provide the greatest opportunity for profit and inventory turnover. Your sales staff is embarrassed if they are not readily available. Even if your overall service level goal is 95 percent, the standard for A-ranked products should be higher. Carefully examine the replenishment parameters of any A-ranked product that has a service level of less than 98 percent or has had more than one stockout within the past 60 days. C-ranked products (typically responsible for the last 5 percent of activity) might have a service level goal of about 90 percent to result in an overall customer service level of 95 percent.

Vendor – Is your customer service level for specific vendors' products unacceptably low? Or are many of their products out of stock for prolonged periods of time? Can you work with these vendors to provide more consistent deliveries and improved product availability?

Buyer – Some buyers are savvier than others. The customer service level and stockout analysis are good objective measurements of a buyer's performance.

Inventory Turnover

While customer service level is probably the most important inventory measurement, turnover is often the most misunderstood. Clear up this misunderstanding and help all your employees realize the true value of inventory turnover. To start, replace the term "inventory turnover" with "opportunity to earn a profit." When talk turns to "inventory turnover" during sales meetings, many people yawn. But if we go into the same meetings and discuss "opportunities to earn a profit," salespeople sit up and pay attention – even though we're addressing the exact same thing.

The concept of inventory turnover is best illustrated with an example. You sell $10,000 worth of a product (at cost) each year. Total revenue received from sales of the product is $12,500. If we bought the entire $10,000 worth of product on January 1, at the end of the year we would have made a $2,500 gross profit on an investment of $10,000.

What if we bought $5,000 worth of the product on January 1? Then, just before running out of stock, we bought an additional $5,000 worth of product with part of the revenues received from selling the first shipment. At the end of the year, we've still sold $10,000 worth of the product, still made $2,500 gross profit, but at any one time we had a maximum of $5,000 invested in inventory.

Could we make the same gross profit on an even smaller investment? What if we bought $2,500 worth of material? Sell most of it. Buy another $2,500 of the product. Sell most of that shipment and then repeat the process two more times before the end of the year. The annual gross profit of $2,500 is now generated with a maximum of $2,500 invested in inventory at one time.

Which investment option is better? Selling $10,000 worth of a product (and making $2,500 gross profit) with an investment of $10,000, $5,000 or $2,500? Investing $2,500 rather than $10,000 frees up $7,500 that can be used for other purposes, such as stocking other products that have the potential of generating additional profits.

Every time we sell an amount of a product, product line or other group of items equal to the average amount of money we have invested in those items, we have "turned" our inventory. The inventory turnover rate measures the number of times we have turned our inventory during the past 12 months.

We use the following formula to calculate inventory turnover:

$$\frac{\text{Cost of goods sold from stock sales during the past 12 months}}{\text{Average inventory investment during the past 12 months}}$$

However, be careful how you determine the cost of goods sold for the overall inventory turnover. You only want to include the value of material actually delivered to customers. If you include the value of material transferred between locations or the value of inventory used in assembling kits, you may exaggerate your company's overall inventory turnover.

If you want to measure the turnover of total inventory in a central warehouse or distribution center, including transfers, do it as a separate measurement. Your actual turnover should only be based on stock sales. In most manufacturing and assembly environments we calculate turnover separately for raw materials (including components) and finished goods.

There are several other things you should keep in mind when calculating turnover rates:

- Only consider cost of goods sold from stock sales that are filled from warehouse inventory. Non-stock items and direct shipments are not included. These sales are important but don't involve your warehouse stock (i.e., your investment in inventory).
- Inventory turnover is based on the cost of items (what you paid for them) not sales dollars (what you sold them for)
- If the cost of products drastically fluctuates due to market conditions, consider basing turnover calculations on weight or cubic volume of product rather than cost. This will allow for better comparisons of performance over time.

The inventory turnover equation includes the average value of stocked inventory. To determine your average inventory investment:

1. Calculate the total value of every product in inventory (quantity on hand times cost) on the last day of every month. Be consistent in using the same cost basis (e.g., average cost, last cost, replacement cost, etc.) in calculating both the cost of goods sold and average inventory investment used to determine inventory

turnover.

2. If your inventory value tends to fluctuate significantly throughout each month, calculate the total inventory value on the first and 15th of every month.

3. Determine the average inventory value by averaging all inventory valuations recorded during the past 12 months.

A turnover rate of six turns per year doesn't mean that the stock of every item will turn six times. The stock of popular, fast-moving items should turn more often (up to 12 or more times per year); the inventory of slow-moving items may turn only once or not at all.

It's a good idea to calculate turnover separately for each vendor line in each warehouse every month. This allows you to identify situations in which your inventory is not providing an adequate return on investment. Inventory turnover will improve as you start buying the "best buy" quantity of each product and liquidating your inventory of dead stock and excess material.

Turn/Earn Index

If a company enjoys high gross margins, it can be successful with lower inventory turns. Many surplus houses justify keeping items in their warehouses for years because they bought the material for pennies on the dollar and will eventually sell some of it for a premium. The turn/earn index will help you balance turnover and profits. It is calculated by multiplying inventory turns by the gross margin percentage. It highlights situations where high margins can compensate for low inventory turns.

For example, if you turn over inventory of an item four times a year and earn an average 30 percent gross margin on each product sale, that's a T/E index of 120. The same return on investment value is achieved if we turn the inventory of an item only twice but make an average gross margin of 60 percent on every sale:

2 turns x 60% average margin = 120 T/E Index

On the other hand, the stock of a product with an average margin of 20 percent has to turnover six times in order to achieve the same 120 T/E index. Your T/E target should normally be at least 120 (e.g., a vendor line turning six times annually and earning an average 20 percent margin). But the higher the T/E index, the better.

Gross Margin Return on Investment (GMROI)

A similar measurement to the T/E Index is gross margin return on investment (GMROI), which also measures the profitability of investment in inventory. GMROI is calculated by dividing gross profit dollars from sales in the past 12 months by the average inventory investment over the same time period:

$$\frac{\text{Gross profit dollars from past 12 months}}{\text{Average inventory value}}$$

For example, if you earned $20,000 in gross profits from an average inventory investment of $10,000, GMROI would be 200 ($20,000 ÷ $10,000 = 2.00). In other words you are earning $2 for every dollar invested in inventory.

While the T/E index and GMROI both measure profitability, they do so based on two different scales (sort of like Fahrenheit and centigrade temperatures). Compare the calculated T/E Index and GMROI using the following data:

12-Month Sales Dollars	$8,000
12-Month Cost of Goods Sold Dollars	$6,000
12-Month Gross Profit Dollars	$2,000
Gross Margin ($2,000 ÷ $8,000)	25%
Average Inventory Value	$2,500
Turnover = ($6,000 ÷ $2,500)	2.4 Turns per Year

$$\text{T/E Index} = 2.4 * 25\% = 60$$
$$\text{GMROI} = 2,000 ÷ \$2,500 = 80$$

Because they utilize different scales, the GMROI will always be greater than the corresponding T/E index.

Three-Way Ranking

For many distributors, 80 percent of sales are generated by no more than 10 percent to 13 percent of their inventory items. In addition, 95 percent of sales are generated by no more than 50 percent of stocked products. Ranking is the process of classifying products to identify those with the most potential.

Typically we use these rankings:

- A-ranked items are responsible for the top 80 percent of activity in the past 12 months.
- B-ranked items are responsible for the next 15 percent of activity in the past 12 months.
- C-ranked items are responsible for the last 5 percent of activity in the past 12 months.
- X-ranked items are dead, that is they have had no activity in the past 12 months.

Most computer systems rank products based on cost of goods sold. But to achieve a complete analysis of your inventory, add two other ranking criteria:

- Number of times the product was sold, transferred or otherwise used in the past 12 months (also known as "hits").
- The profitability of the item.

Each ranking is used for a different purpose. To achieve our potential inventory turnover, carefully determine the reorder quantities of the items with the most dollars moving through inventory. These are the A-ranked products based on cost of goods sold. At the same time, consider maintaining additional safety stock for products with a high hit rank to minimize the chance of stock outs. Let salespeople and management know what products are generating the most profits. These are the A items based on profitability.

Categorizing each product utilizing all three ranks provides a comprehensive analysis that no single ranking can provide. For example, product A100 is assigned an A rank based on annual cost of goods sold. But a three-way ranking provides a more complete picture:

COGS Rank	Hits Rank	Profitability Rank
A	A	C

This is a product that is ordered frequently by customers and has a lot of dollars moving through inventory but does not generate a lot of profits. This may be a loss leader that should drive additional profitable sales.

Consider the three-way ranking of another product assigned an A rank based on annual cost of goods sold:

COGS Rank	Hits Rank	Profitability Rank
A	C	A

This is a much more profitable item, but it experiences fewer hits. Ask your salespeople if anything can be done to encourage more sales of this product.

What would the ranking of your best products look like? Consider the three-way ranking for the following item:

COGS Rank	Hits Rank	Profitability Rank
C	A	A

This is a highly profitable item that is sold quite often. But because it is low in cost, it does not require a high dollar investment.

Ranking products based only on hits and/or annual cost of goods sold provides an incomplete picture of inventory performance. Three-way ranking provides valuable information concerning each stocked product's contribution to the overall profitability of an organization –

information that is vital in your quest to achieve effective inventory management.

Day's Supply of Inventory

Often it is difficult to find a measurement of inventory performance that is meaningful to everyone in an organization. In many cases day's supply of inventory can provide this much needed metric. Day's supply of inventory is calculated by dividing the current available inventory of an item by the forecasted demand per day.

For example, the available quantity of item #R600 is 1,000 pieces and usage is forecast at five pieces per day. This represents a 200-day supply of the item:

$$\frac{\textbf{1,000 pieces}}{\textbf{5 pieces per day}} = \textbf{200-Day Supply}$$

We have found that salespeople, buyers, warehouse people and especially upper-level management can relate easily to this measurement.

Excess Inventory

Many financial institutions recognize the importance of turning over the inventory of products that do sell. They do not look at the value of dead stock but are more concerned with excess inventory. Excess inventory is defined as any quantity of a product in excess of "x" month's supply. The value of x varies by industry. For example, industrial distributors often use a 12-month supply in this calculation while food distributors usually work with a three-month supply as their excess point.

For example, a distributor has sold 10 pieces of a B200 widget during the past 12 months. It has 15 pieces in stock. As a result five pieces, would be considered to be excess stock. For new items without sales in previous months, use the projected sales over the next x months in determining excess inventory.

Not all dead stock is part of your excess inventory value. If you've sold none in the last 12 months, any quantity you have on hand is more than what is needed. Best-practice companies try to limit the value of their excess stock to 5 percent to 10 percent of their total inventory value.

Implications for Action

Achieving effective inventory management is not easy. But in today's environment of more competition and additional customer demands of product availability, it is a critical component of success. Use the metrics discussed in this chapter to measure your progress in maximizing the profitability and productivity of what is probably your organization's largest asset.

Action Steps: Inventory Management Analytics

- Ensure salespeople are accurately recording promise dates and other customer requests for each line of an order to more precisely determine whether your company is meeting, exceeding or falling short of expectations.

- Carefully examine replenishment parameters for your A-ranked products with a service level below 98 percent or with more than one stockout during the last 60 days. These are the products your customers request most, so they have the greatest opportunity for profit – if you have them when you need them.

- Change the conversation so employees pay more attention to inventory turnover. Replace that term with "opportunity to earn a profit."

- Calculate your company's Turn/Earn Index, which helps balance turnover and profits, by multiplying inventory turns by gross margin percentage. Aim for a T/E index of at least 120.

- Analyze and share day's supply of inventory, a measurement your entire workforce from the C-suite to the sales team to the warehouse will understand. Calculate this by dividing the current available inventory of an item by the forecasted demand per day.

About the Author

Jon Schreibfeder is president of Effective Inventory Management, Inc., a firm dedicated to helping manufacturers, distributors and large retailers get the most out of their investment in stock inventory. For more than 20 years, Jon has served as an inventory management consultant to over two thousand firms to improve their productivity and profitability through better inventory management. Learn more at www.effectiveinventory.com.

Chapter 9

Next Steps:
Build Your Analytics Capability

Thomas P. Gale, MDM Analytics

Our intention with this book was twofold. First, we wanted to provide a snapshot of how and where leading distribution companies in 2015 are applying analytics to improve their bottom lines. We hope one or more of these chapters resonated as a specific area to strengthen a weakness, capitalize on opportunity or improve financial and operational performance. Specific analytic projects can yield quick and meaningful impacts, as well as evergreen returns for a company.

Second, we hope this collection of some of the best analytic thinking in distribution motivates you to increase analytics capability within your organization to build a stronger decision making process. Our contributing authors are passionate about the outcomes they have seen in companies that increase analytics capabilities. You can transform your business into a higher performance company by implementing the analytical best practices outlined here.

You can bring in consultants or hired-gun data specialists for one-off or high-priority projects, but the rapidly shifting competitive landscape in distribution requires that every company develop an analytics champion. The job description will vary widely, but every distribution company must cultivate skills and experience in the more effective use of their business data.

What's Next in Analytics?

This book has presented examples of the different descriptive, predictive and prescriptive analytics that leading distributors are using today. But it is not comprehensive. For example, we did not address human resources analytics, yet with the current challenges distributors face in hiring, retaining and developing talent, this is an increasingly important arena where analytics can help companies optimize their processes.

Some aspects of "big data" are covered in this current edition, as several chapters outline how daily line-item detail in aggregated form over months or years can yield extremely valuable analytic insights into purchasing patterns and behavior. Another definition of big data not covered in this edition centers on the analysis of unstructured data, such as social media, email and website user data and content.

Big data analytics of unstructured digital data is rapidly emerging as the frontier where the largest and most technologically invested distributors are now focusing efforts as they expand their reach from B2B to B2C and into much wider end-market customer and geographic segments.

The field of analytics is exploding, and we intend to update this book periodically as the use of analytics in distribution evolves. This is a fascinating time of transition in technology and data in wholesale distribution, evidenced by the explosive growth in the tools available to distributors across the spectrum of analytics. As our 2014 research determined, the tools currently outweigh analytics capabilities in the vast majority of distribution companies.

To benchmark current capabilities, use the assessment tool in **Figure 9-1** on page 125. Then start the journey to build increasing analytics thinking and capability into an organization in the years ahead.

Write the Road Map

Here are some steps to transition to a more analytic thinking organization:

1. **Benchmark current analytics status.** Share this book across your organization, not only the current leaders but the emerging leaders of tomorrow. Discuss the book and evaluate level of enthusiasm and consensus. Use the chart at the end of this chapter to assess current use of data across the spectrum of basic reporting to more predictive analytics. Is there a potential champion that could carry the analytics torch forward?

2. **Identify gaps and priorities.** Using the chapters of this book, what analytics will move the needle for your unique situation? Quantify the impact of specific analytics activities and projects. Build a project wish list with due dates and budget estimates.

3. **Document a vision and road map.** This is a critical step many companies don't address. What will it take to create an analytics culture, where analytic thinking is nurtured and elevated as a core process and competency? How long? What are the first steps?

4. **Define the talent required.** Consider your current roster. Is there a skills gap that can be bridged with professional development? As you evaluate new hires and management team needs, carefully consider the analytic thinking that candidates can add to your team.

5. **Create and execute an analytics plan.** Boil the above steps into an action plan with deadlines and accountability. Be intentional about transforming your decision-making processes with a strengthening foundation in analytics, and ultimately into an analytic thinking culture.

6. **Use www.distributorsguide.com/analytics**, the resource page for this book, as an evolving resource guide. You'll find links to many books and other resources to advance the analytics learning in your organization.

These steps will position your company to mine the current analytics gap that exists in wholesale distribution today. The sooner you elevate the role that data and analytics plays in your company, as part of the day-to-day conversation, the more control you will take for building your company's competitive advantage and destiny.

Better business decisions with analytics

The capabilities assessment template on the next page provides a grid to first determine the relative importance of specific analytic capabilities discussed in this book and beyond, based on a ranking system of 0 to 5, with 5 being most important. Then grade your company's current performance (A-F) to identify individual capabilities or broader areas that may require focus and resources. It is by no means comprehensive; add more specific detail as applies to your business.

Figure 9-1: Analytics Capabilities Assessment

Importance (5=most important)		Grade
	Financial/Operations	
5 4 3 2 1 0	Custom reporting	A B C D F
5 4 3 2 1 0	Dashboards	A B C D F
5 4 3 2 1 0	Gross margin	A B C D F
5 4 3 2 1 0	Net profit	A B C D F
5 4 3 2 1 0	Cost to serve	A B C D F
5 4 3 2 1 0	Return on assets	A B C D F
5 4 3 2 1 0	Pricing	A B C D F
5 4 3 2 1 0	Other operational data	A B C D F
	Supply Chain	
5 4 3 2 1 0	Inventory optimization	A B C D F
5 4 3 2 1 0	Supplier performance	A B C D F
5 4 3 2 1 0	Branch efficiency	A B C D F
5 4 3 2 1 0	Truck routing	A B C D F
	Human Resources	
5 4 3 2 1 0	Compensation plans	A B C D F
5 4 3 2 1 0	Job performance	A B C D F
5 4 3 2 1 0	Skills assessment	A B C D F
5 4 3 2 1 0	Professional development	A B C D F
	Marketing & Sales	
5 4 3 2 1 0	Market profiling	A B C D F
5 4 3 2 1 0	Customer profiling	A B C D F
5 4 3 2 1 0	Competitive factors	A B C D F
5 4 3 2 1 0	New products/services	A B C D F
5 4 3 2 1 0	Value documentation	A B C D F
5 4 3 2 1 0	Lifecycle management	A B C D F
5 4 3 2 1 0	Promotion targeting	A B C D F
5 4 3 2 1 0	Web/digital metrics	A B C D F
5 4 3 2 1 0	Sales process/stages	A B C D F
5 4 3 2 1 0	Account targeting	A B C D F

About Gale Media, Inc

Gale Media is a market-leading information services and publishing company. Its two business units – Modern Distribution Management and MDM Analytics (formerly Industrial Market Information) – provide knowledge products and services to professionals in industrial product and wholesale distribution markets.

Since 1967, MDM has been the definitive resource for distribution management best practices, competitive intelligence and market trends through its twice-monthly newsletter, market intelligence reports, books and conferences.

MDM Analytics provides proprietary market research and analytic services to profile market share and account potential for industrial products.

For more information, visit www.mdm.com.